The International Military Collectors Guide

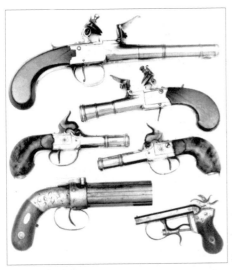

The International Military Collectors Guide

Gary Sterne

ARMS AND ARMOUR

Irene Moore

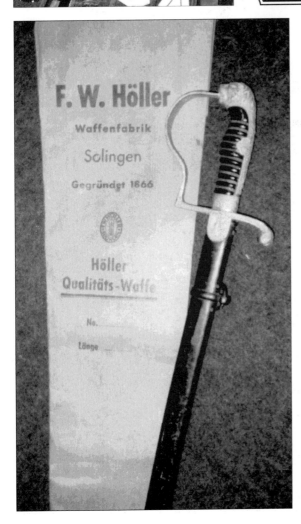

F. W. Höller

Waffenfabrik

Solingen

Gegründet 1866

Höller Qualitäts-Waffe

No.

Länge

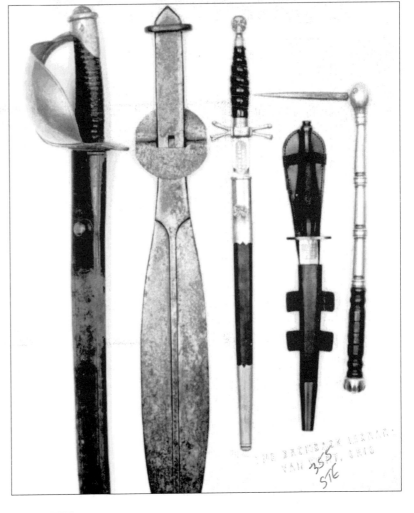

Arms and Armour Press
An Imprint of the Cassell Group,
Wellington House,
125 Strand, London WC2R 0BB.

Distributed in the USA by
Sterling Publishing Co. Inc.,
387 Park Avenue South,
New York, NY 10016-8810.

British Library
Cataloguing-in-Publication Data:
a catalogue record for this book
is available from the British Library.

ISBN 1-85409-419-X

Designed by Gary Sterne.

Printed and bound in Great Britain.

CONTENTS

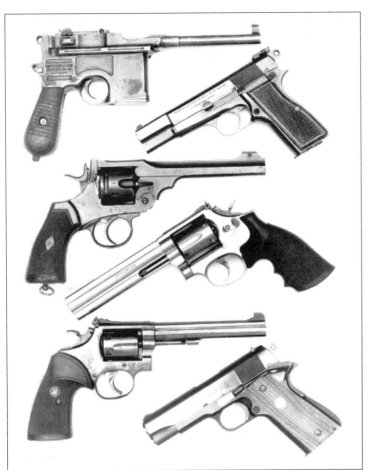

ACKNOWLEDGEMENTS

Photographs - Pat Sterne • Ron Brigden • Robert Attard • Jose Miguel Gallego • M. Mitton
Les Stillman • R. Mitchell • Wallis & Wallis auctioneers • Weller & Dufty auctioneers.

The authors acknowledge with thanks the assistance given by:

Andrew Taylor – uniforms, head-dress

Paul Laidlaw – uniforms

Graham Maddocks – head-dress

John Carlin – ordnance

John Anderson – equipment

Norman Litchfield – badges

Richmond Dutton – edged weapons, miscellaneous

Ray Westlake – books

Peter Duckers – medals

Garth Vincent – edged weapons, firearms

And of course the many hundreds of dealers who have allowed us to photograph their items
without whom this book would not have been possible.

INTRODUCTION

We all enjoy collecting, some of us more enthusiastically and with greater discrimination than others. Whether the object of interest is a rare botanical species, a great work of art, or (as in our case) an elusive frog for an unusual pattern of bayonet, the true collector will be prepared to expend what to some might appear to be disproportionate amounts of time, energy and money on the quest. The collector of militaria is no exception and the areas of interest revealed at militaria fairs and shows worldwide prove to be as varied and intriguing as the collectors themselves. There are those whose speciality is whittled down to the narrowest of fields: "I only go for the 3rd Left Boot Battalion of the 2nd Hindustani Rifles." These are the collectors who seem fated to frequent disappointments and whose wistful "Nothing for me here today" as they leave an event makes one wish that they would cast their net wider. Others, however, come away delighted with some new acquisition, whether it be a rusted battlefield relic, a long sought-after cloth patch, a highly priced medal to a long-dead hero or a cavalry sword with impeccable Waterloo provenance.

For these are the objects that illuminate history and bring it to life in our hands. To handle the rough red woollen cloth of a Georgian coatee and know that it faded in the blistering sun of Portugal, to feel the weight of a Cromwellian lobster-tailed helmet and imagine facing a charge by Prince Rupert, or to balance the length of a Martini-Henry rifle and remember the steadfast lines at Rorke's Drift...these inanimate articles cannot fail to fire the imagination.

Prosaically, they also reveal much about battlefield life and the study of military history. After all, if war is 80 per cent boredom, 15 per cent exhaustion and 5 per cent sheer terror, the artefacts associated with the monotonous parts are just as valid in depicting a way of life. Re-enactors of all periods of history understand this fact and strive for maximum authenticity in creating their camps. Visitors to an American Civil War encampment may find the resting participants consuming pork and beans prepared in a dixie as it would have been prior to the battle of Gettysburg – no camping gas for the true re-enactor!

Camp kettles, kitbags, mess tins and the soldier's 'housewife' are therefore in a way as useful in revealing the past realities of military life as are blade, bayonet and firearm.

Family heirlooms also play their part in bringing history to life and will be treasured for their personal worth rather than their intrinsic value as collectable items. A First World War pair or trio of medals can be bought for a small sum at any collectors' event; and, ironically, the medals which great-grandfather earned in years of footslogging may be cherished by his descendants even more than he valued them himself.

Most people have at least one family member with a military connection and researching a family tree can lead to a quest for more information and the medals, uniforms, paperwork and the like that help to flesh out the facts. So family history may be the first spark to ignite the fuse of a collecting explosion. Then, having experienced the anticipation of discovering something of significant value, the collector is hooked.

Because information is the currency of collectors, research and shared knowledge with like-minded enthusiasts provide much of the enjoyment. Military collectors' clubs, re-enacting societies, the

Part of the Steel Tower at the Royal Armouries in Leeds

Military Vehicle Trust and other organisations, bring collectors together and play an important part in passing on and collating information and preserving items for future generations to enjoy.

Conservation and restoration are subjects that occasion much heart-searching by collectors – for where does the former end and the latter begin? It could be argued that in the case of any antique we are merely custodians or guardians for a time – in some cases a lifetime – and then the item is passed on to another generation. It makes sense then that it should be passed on in good condition and not allowed to deteriorate any further. Whether to go beyond that is a subject for a book in itself. As one experienced collector of pickelhauben put it: 'No one would ever seek to darn the hole in Admiral Nelson's jacket, but they might want to clean off 190 years of dust and stop it being eaten by 20th-century moths!'

Having started a collection, however small, there is great pleasure to be had from displaying it. Collections of military items have been accumulated as long as man has carried weapons. In lawless pre-civilised times certain weapons were intended to be borne at all times, both for ceremonial and practical use, but others too heavy and impractical to be carried were attached to the walls of great halls – an Anglo-Saxon two-handed throwing axe, for example, would have made uncomfortable everyday wear. Thus developed the

Part of a symmetrical display at Culzean Castle near Ayr

tradition of weaponry displays which served the combined purpose of attesting to military strength and providing a practical means of storage.

Over the centuries, as the need to carry weapons receded, wall displays became more formalised, fantastic designs being created from edged weapons and firearms. This led to the sort of vandalism which appals today's enthusiasts as weapons were cut down in order to not to spoil the artistic symmetry of a particular pattern. An example of this can be seen at Culzean Castle near Ayr, Scotland, whose armoury contains 729 flintlock pistols, 400 swords, more than a hundred bayonets, two great clusters of light dragoon holster pistols and a lattice created of truncated hanger swords collected and arranged by the Victorian 3rd Marquess of Ailsa.

The new Royal Armouries Museum at Leeds, in northern England, has re-created this ancient theme of weapons on display. The museum's centrepiece is a 100-foot Tower of Steel and on the walls of the hollow inner octagon are displayed more than 3000 pieces of mainly 17th-century armour and 19th-century equipment.

Collectors with more modest space at their disposal have to be satisfied with less lavish displays – a loft conversion, a spare room or even a cupboard or box. While the décor of a modern home does not often lend itself to shows of military weaponry, an attractive display cabinet of medals or insignia might be considered, and some items can be stored outside – the garden of a French home on the Somme contains an effective array of battlefield relics from the Great War.

Militaria collectors today are following in an ancient tradition and paying their own tribute to the warriors of the past, whether from battlefields centuries ago or from those within living memory. Thanks to their efforts, objects that might have been discarded are preserved for future generations to handle – and wonder at the stories that lie behind these tangible remnants of history.

Relic weapons and equipment on show outside a guesthouse on the Somme

ABOUT THIS BOOK

The aim of this book is to provide a practical guide to the range and diversity of militaria available for collection and the level of market prices that items are currently fetching. The photographs were gathered by The Armourer – a magazine for militaria collectors worldwide, based in the UK.

It will soon become apparent that the photographs concerned are not posed 'studio' shots. With a few exceptions, they were taken, over a period of three years, in the hustle and bustle of arms and militaria fairs in the UK, USA and Europe, and they feature items which were on sale on dealers' stalls. Sometimes we were able to take the items away and photograph them in a quieter, more favourable setting, but more often than not the pictures were taken in crowded rooms with less than perfect lighting. As a result, some are of mixed quality and composition. The authors and publisher have chosen to include these images so as to maximise the range of items shown.

These so-called fairs' pictures were published bi-monthly in The Armourer and proved a popular and invaluable guide to market prices for both collectors and dealers. This unique source of hundreds of pictures of militaria and the prices being asked for them is now available to the collector in book form.

Whereas auction catalogues and price guides provide a useful indication of value, this book differs in the information it offers to collectors. It provides pictures and prices of many smaller inexpensive items, of great interest to collectors, but often consigned to auction job lots and therefore not priced individually. It also furnishes 'market' prices i.e. not an artificial value placed on something but the actual price at which the dealer was selling.

A word about price: in militaria, as in any field of antiques, it is important to remember that the cost of an item largely depends on its rarity, provenance and condition – but there are other less tangible variables that also affect price to a greater or lesser extent.

First and most importantly, the price depends quite simply on whether you are buying or selling. Collectors often forget this when they come to sell an item from their collection and are disappointed at the price offered by a dealer. It is as well to remember that the average dealer is a businessman who makes his living by making a profit on the items he sells. He has overheads he must meet – at a militaria fair these will include, at the very least, the cost of his table or booth, his travelling expenses and perhaps hotel accommodation. Larger dealers will have shop premises and staff to pay, and will spend time and money travelling around the world in search of unusual pieces.

Second, the price of an item for sale may depend on how much the purchaser wishes to pay, how good at haggling he or she is and what sort of a day the vendor is having! A dealer on day three of a large military show who has made a good profit and is looking forward to loading up and getting home may be more receptive to offers than one who has just arrived for the start of an event and has yet to discover how well the day will go.

Buying and selling at auction can also produce some surprises and is subject to another set of variables. The price an item is estimated to fetch frequently bears little relation to its eventual hammer price as competition in the auction room hots up among keen buyers. Equally, a poor attendance or several of the same type of item in the sale, may result in lower bids.

Collectors wishing to buy and sell items should be prepared to do their homework first, and this volume is offered as a useful 'text book'. Each section deals with a different aspect of militaria collecting such as uniforms, headgear, edged weapons, firearms, etc. Within each section there are pictures of items to suit every budget – from a magnificent Garde du Corps helmet at £3500 to a humble piece of cloth insignia worth about £1. In between there are hundreds of items with brief descriptions and the price asked by the vendor.

Also, just a short note about the annotations on some of the photographs. In most instances a price is shown and it has been displayed in the currency of the particular vendor.

On some pictures a code of **NPA** (no price available) has been shown – this is generally because the vendor was unable or unwilling to set a price when the photograph was taken. He may have just acquired the item and still be considering what it might fetch. Since many of the NPA items are of interest to collectors despite not having a fixed price, they are reproduced here.

The majority of pictures within the Western Front Relic pages have no price. Obviously some of these items are purely for display or were found and are difficult to value, once again they are included as useful reference and hopefully indicate something of the quantity and quality of this type of item.

	£1.00	Sterling
Approximate	1.64	US Dollars
	2.78	DM
MONETARY	9.60	French Francs
EXCHANGE RATES	2.36	Spanish Pesetas
	7.31	South African Rand
at the time of going to press	2.16	Australian dollars
	0.63	Maltese pounds
	9585.33	Russian roubles

To list all the vendors would be impractical, but if you spot the piece you have been searching for years, please write to:-
The Armourer Magazine,
25 Westbrook Drive, Macclesfield, Cheshire, SK10 3AQ, UK.
stating the item and the page number – and where possible, we will put you in touch with the person who was selling it.

HEAD-DRESS

Over the centuries, the need to protect the head during combat or campaign has resulted in an astonishing diversity of solutions – from the steel and leather-padded helm of the armoured knight to the simple cloth beret of the Second World War, from the gloriously impractical Imperial Prussian 'Garde du Corps' helmet, with its winged eagle, to the harsh reality of the German M16 steel helmet.

It is not surprising, therefore, that head-dress is one of the most popular categories of militaria collecting, offering almost limitless choice and with prices to suit every budget. Like all clothing, hats retain something of the wearer and there can be as much merit in a well-worn item as in one which appears to have just been issued.

The earliest and most expensive items to collect are the armoured helms of the 15th, 16th and 17th centuries – rarely seen outside museums. There are, however, some good Victorian copies to be found and even modern miniature armours, correct in every detail, which offer a less expensive alternative. More often seen in the UK, both at fairs and at auction, are the 'lobster-tailed' helmets of the English Civil War period, with their characteristic flared neck guard.

To the collector of head-dress, the Napoleonic Wars of the late 18th and early 19th centuries offer a wonderful diversity of style. Never in the field of human conflict was so much gold and silver lace, braid, fur, feathers, gilt buttons and trimming worn by so many for making war. Grenadier bearskin caps with silvered plates, high-topped shakos with beautifully coloured plumes, crested helmets topped with fur combs – the selection is huge, and so are many of the prices. However, head-dress prices continue to rise and collectors buying as an investment can feel fairly confident that their asset will increase in value.

The Imperial German pickelhaube or spiked helmet is an extremely popular collectors' item. Introduced in 1842 and re-designed many times, the pickelhaube can be seen at most militaria fairs. It remained in military service until the First World War – long enough to be produced in large numbers – and as it carried a wide variety of unit decorations, and was produced in so many different forms and variations, the pickelhaube itself offers a lifetime of study to some collectors.

So popular was the pickelhaube that it spawned imitations in other European nations, one of the most notable being the British blue cloth helmet introduced in 1879, of which many examples are to be found today.

Although the use of armour died out in the 17th century, metal helmets in one form or another have continued to be worn by many nations. During the First World War, German doctors treating so many soldiers with head wounds as a result of trench warfare began to campaign for better head protection. This resulted in the development of the classic M16 German steel helmet which is now so sought after by collectors.

Steel helmets of all nationalities abound – the French Adrian helmet, for example, with its characteristic 'comb', of which more than three million were made and distributed before the end of 1915. The Adrian is usually more moderately priced than many other First World War helmets and is also to be found with many different paint shades, badges, liner formats and chinstraps because of the varied uses to which it was put – after the First World War it was worn by Chinese, Japanese, Hungarian, Polish, Belgian and Italian troops. Even German auxiliary workers such as air raid wardens wore captured Adrian helmets with German badges, so it is worth looking out for the more unusual variants.

British 'Tommy' helmets from the First World War are available at reasonable prices, and here, too, collectors look out for the unusual ones, perhaps with interesting contemporary modifications such as an officer's-pattern chinstrap or an other ranks helmet or cap, a rarely encountered helmet cover or even one with an experimental chain mesh visor. Just occasionally, real gems turn up, such as the puzzling First World War trenchcap without leather trimmings which turned out to belong to a Hindu member of an Indian regiment.

The Second World War period offers an enormous spectrum of hats, caps and helmets with, as a general rule, German and paratroop items fetching the highest prices. S.S. hats, Afrika Korps caps and British, German and American paratroop helmets are all popular items and appear at militaria events. As in many aspects of collecting, there are some clever fakes around, so the buyer should beware.

Post-war, Vietnam, Falklands, Gulf War and current UN headgear, some of which sell today for pocket-money prices, will no doubt be fetching high prices in years to come, so, like a wine connoisseur, perhaps it might be worth laying down a stock of these items now for the middle of the next century.

FURTHER READING:

German Uniforms of the Third Reich
Brian L. Davis
Arms and Armour Press

Civil War Uniforms
Philip J. Haythornthwaite,
Arms and Armour Press

Napoleon's Line Cavalry
Stephen E. Maughan
Windrow & Greene

Prussian Pickelhaube (Maltese £). **£200**
Prussian (refinished) Cuirassier helmet (Maltese £) **£450**

WWI 2nd pattern helmet, with khaki finish **£65**

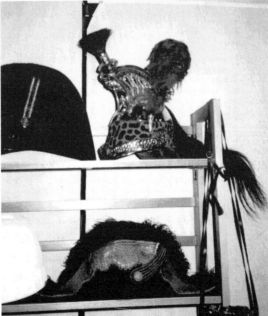

Top: Napoleon III Dragoon helmet 1854 . . . . **12,000 FF**
General's bicorne hat. Napoleon III c. 1860 with epaulettes and belt . . . . **8,500 FF**

Other ranks sealskin cap to the Isle of Wight Rifles
1908-1915 . . . . **£175**
Wing epaulettes to the Black Watch.
Pre Crimean War **£175**

Various hats, British Navy, Russian Army, Navy,
Irish Guards and Scots Guards priced from . . **£30**

British WW2 Para Regiment beret, including
period badge **£65**

Lance cap to 5th Royal Irish . . . . **NPA**

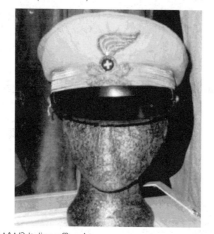

WW2 Italian officer's cap
(Pioneer or Engineers) **£95**

WW1 British, WW2 German field caps, Russian
infantry cap, American side cap, Canadian soft hat,
various prices. German Feldmütze **£75**

Black Swiss WW1 fire brigade helmet **£145**
1950's white Danish fire brigade helmet **£150**
German S.S. camouflage helmet with cover . . . **£175**

Imperial German Shako **£350**
Felt Pickelhaube **£275**
German M1916 steel helmet **£130**
Other assorted headwear . . . . **NPA**

Peaked caps from . . . . **£25 to £35**

Tarlatan to Northamptonshire Yeomanry.
Napoleonic War period **£2,500**

Miscellaneous Guards caps from **£15**

Russian Colonel's winter hat including hammer and sickle enamel badge.
Excellent condition **£45**

Various German WW2 hats
1938 S.S. visor cap, named to owner **$1,870**
S.S. visor cap size 56, named to owner **$1,550**
S.S. cap 1933 . . . . **$2,100**
Naval Submarines visor cap U-42 . . . . **$750**

Early pattern 'drop eagle' Flight Section NCO's hat **£245**

Royal Air Force brass bodied drum 1941 . . . . **£150**
Royal Air Force slouch hat WW2 dated **£75**
Royal Australian Air Force slouch hat 1944 . . . . **£65**

Officer's shako 1861-78 of Renfrew Militia **£650**

British Victorian officer's home service helmet to the Volunteer Artillery . . . **£345**
1870's pattern tropical helmet with Victorian helmet plate and spike top . . . **£225**
British Victorian OR's home service helmet to the Yorks & Lancs Rgmt **£245**

Barbados Police helmet **£65**
New Zealand Police helmet **£65**
Greater Manchester W.P.C. cap **£20**

WW2 side caps: including, Army Clergy Officer's side cap, Naval officer's cap, Herman Goring Div. ski cap, Afrika Korps General's ski cap, Field Bishop Afrika Korps . . . . **£500** to **£1,500**

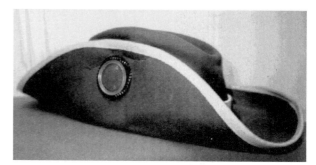

Imperial German slouch hat worn in South West Africa, as denoted by the white band and edging. Schütztrüpen – commanded by Paul Von Lellow-Vorbeck **£150**

French Foreign Legion kepis, current issue. Left. **£58**
Right **£30**
Parade Epaulettes (current issue) **£110**

WW2 assorted flying hats, German net type fighter pilot's helmet **£220**
German fur lined flying helmet **£220**
Luftwaffe Russian front issue **£195**
British B. Type flying helmet with rare D type mask **£975**
British C Type flying helmet.
New unused condition with original packet **£275**

Officer's Blue Cloth helmet to the Bedfordshire Regiment. Silver stags badge on enamel back plate with silver regimental scroll beneath **£650**

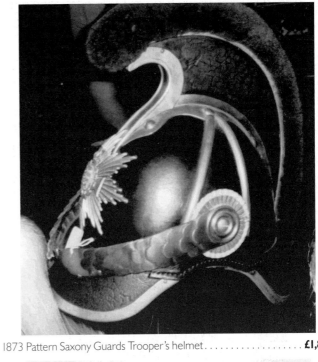

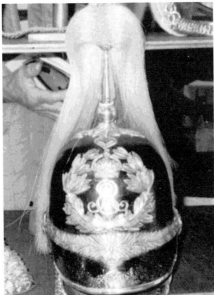

King's Own Norfolk Imperial Yeomanry helmet **£700**

1873 Pattern Saxony Guards Trooper's helmet **£1,865**

Two Yorkshire battlefield relics: an English 3 bar lobster-tailed helmet from the English Civil War period, found at Marston Moor **£200**
A relic dagger from Towton **£85**

Kabuto Helmet, as worn by Samurai warrior, circa EDO period . . . . . . **NPA**

A relic WWII German helmet with some original liner and strap **£20**

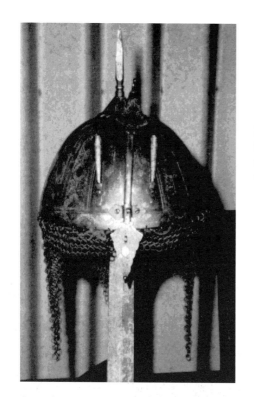

Indo-Persian helmet, finely etched in silver and gold Kula-kud 18th century **£650**

WWII 'First Aid Post' helmet **£30**

German DD Police combat helmet **£485**

Later war raw-edge M42 German helmet with Luftwaffe single decal and Normandy camouflage. **£250**

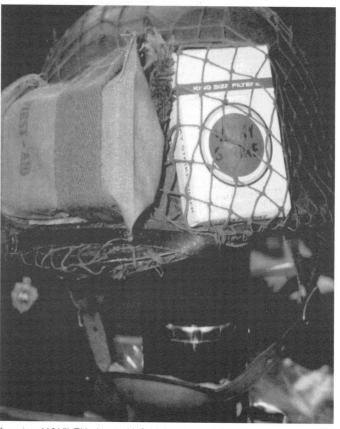

German camouflage helmet cover **£100**

American WWII GI helmet with field dressing and cigarettes **£110**

Luftwaffe helmet, incomplete liner, reasonable condition . . . . **NPA**

Various Helmets: Left to right.

Nazi Fire Police	**£75**
Waffen S.S.	**£410**
Child's helmet.	**N/P**
Para helmet of unknown type	**N/P**
Luftwaffe flight section cap	**£150**
Army cap.	**£120**
Luftwaffe ski cap.	**£115**
Luftwaffe ski cap	**£85**

A rare Victorian Officer's helmet, worn 1853-55, of the Durham Artillery Militia, black PL skull with silver plated copper peak binding, top mount with ball and rose ornamented plume socket, velvet backed chinscales and ear rosettes, silver plated crowned escutcheon HP bearing gilt grenade over crossed cannon, at the foot a scroll inscribed "Durham", padded silk lining, white hair plume, maker's label inside of "Andrews. Helmet Maker etc. to Her Majesty...". In its original japanned tin case and brass nameplate engraved "C.L. Wood Esq, Durham Artillery". Collingwood Lindsay Wood, commissioned 1st Lieutenant July 1853, when the unit was formed.
The helmet was worn from then until 1855 . . . . **£935**

Officer's Saxon Guard Reitcher helmet, circa 1905, with copper and silver furniture. **£4,850**

German Kriegsmarine single decal helmet with spray camouflage 1938 .... **£195**

WW1 American Brodie. Shell only, marked to the 82nd Division **£30**

Belgium WW1 infantry helmet. **£40**

German leather Pickelhaube with brass trim. **£185**

European pattern lobster tailed helmet. **£55**

Luftwaffe double decal paratrooper's helmet with early 'small' Luftwaffe eagle **£1,850**

17th Century Japanese Kabuto (Samurai helmet) signed by maker "YOSHIMICHI" **£2,500**

Kriegsmarine war flag **£180**
Carved wooden plaque to 1st Panzer pioneer corps **£85**
District Nurse enamel station sign **£85**
M18 Helmet re-issued to the S.A. emergency motorcycle
dispatch rider **£650**

Argentine helmet from the Falklands war, early 1980s **£20**

French Gendarmerie helmet. **£425**

Bavarian 1910 Infantry officer's helmet with parade plume **£1,350**
King's Dragoon Guards officer's helmet 1871 . . . . **£1,850**

Belgian Cuirasse in brass circa 1920 . . . . £575

Various German helmets from . . . . £35 – £220

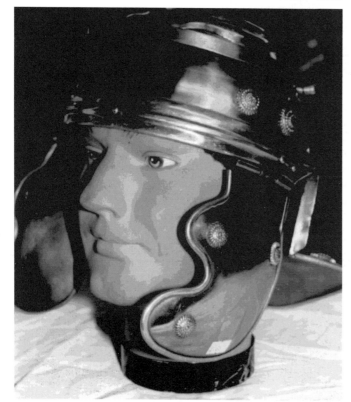

Reproduction Legionnaire's helmet £165

M42 German single decal Luftwaffe. Decal at 100% but leg of swastika stretched **£210**

Selection of helmets and cases:
Volunteer Artillery Officer's **£400**
Victorian Artillery Officer's **£400**
Edwardian Territorial Artillery Officer's **£400**
Edwardian Princess of Wales Yorkshire Regiment **£425**

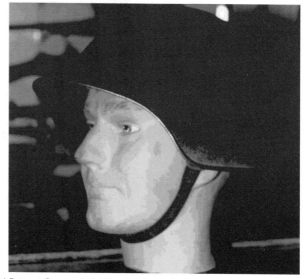

M36 Pattern German WWII undecalled helmet. **£415**

Panzer Grenadier officer's crusher cap **£350**
Luftwaffe ski cap **£130**
Luftwaffe officer's cap **£350**
Luftwaffe combat ground assault wire net helmet **£300**
Baden Pickelhaube . . . **£300**
Kriegsmarine helmet . **£325**
Luftwaffe 2nd Pattern dagger **£300**
Kriegsmarine dagger and straps **£450**

Georgian officer's 1817 pattern helmet of the Household Cavalry, silver plated skull and high comb, with copper gilt acanthus foliage, edging, leather backed ornamental chinscales and ear rosettes, rayed helmet plate bearing Royal Arms and motto on Prince of Wales feathers, with battle honours "Peninsula" and "Waterloo", black bearskin crest, in its original shaped case. **£1,800**
An officer's gilt helmet of The 5th (Princess Charlotte of Wales) Dragoon Guards, gilt mounts, ear to ear wreath, red morocco backed chinchain and ear rosettes, gilt and silver plated HP, padded silk lining, white and red hair plume with small rosette. Gilt generally good **£1,100**

British steel helmet WWII **£12**
Para helmet with chin straps **£120**
as above with leather chin strap **£185**

Ersatz Baden
Pickelhaube 1915
in good condition
with original
gilt wash **£300**

Fife Light Horse Officer's helmet, circa 1895,
with named tin (Hutchison) **£1,150**

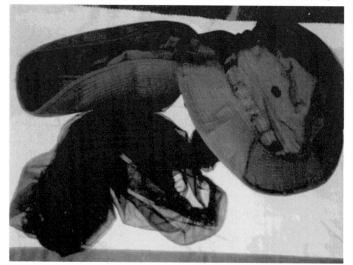

British Nazi Party badge, German Eagle holding S.S. type skull, says 'England
Awake', would appear German manufacture but with British cap badge
loops on back . . . . **US $1,000**

Vietnam dated American jungle hat, with insect net, mint condition **£15**

Scottish feather bonnet to Gordon Highlanders **£175**
Foreign service helmet to Royal Engineers. **£225**
Coldstream Guards bearskin. **£200**
O/R's Pickelhauben. L to R: Würtenburg, Baden, Bavarian . . . **£300** - **£340**

Officer's Blue Cloth helmet to the West Riding Regiment. Victorian. . . . **£450**

Pith helmet which belonged to
Lt. WHC Llewllyn former
Lord Lt. Glamorgan who
served on the NW Frontier
1908-35 . . . . **£85**

USAF Korean P1 Type
flyer's helmet. **£90**

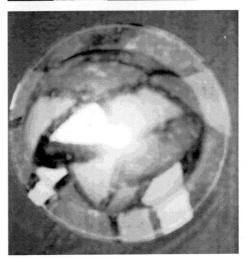

U.S. Tommy Hat,
camouflaged in
WWI style, cond.
fair. . . . . **US $150**

Reproduction Helmets:
Burgonet **£195**
Helmet with nasal guard. **£65**
"Pig Face" **£95**

French WWI experimental visor helmet, 2nd pattern, 1915 . . . . **£500**

Nazi period Fire Police helmet, complete with leather neck shield and leather liner **£95**

WWI Prussian officer's Pickelhaube with carrying case and combat cover. Helmet also has an inlaid silk interior. **£650**

Russian headwear. Naval cap. **£55**
Standard issue heavyweight flying helmet **£75**
Early style field cap **£45**
1940 pattern steel helmet **£55**
Officer's peaked cap. **£55**
Cossack hat. **£75**

Reproduction helmets:
Trojan helmet **£140**
Barbouza **£95**

NCO Mountain troops cap. **£350**
Officer's 17th Regiment cap. **£375**
Luftwaffe double decal helmet **£375**
Nazi police shako. **£250**

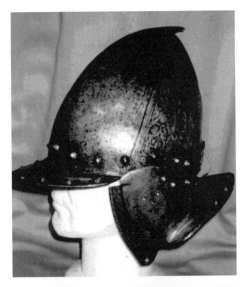

Bourgenet, circa 1560-1700. Etched and with pear shaped finial, ear flaps and brass plume holder. Milan Workshop **£1,600**

U.S. 78th Division helmet. . . . . **1,000 FF**

Barbados Police Officer's helmet. **£65**

Victorian Blue Cloth helmet to the Volunteer Artillery, with silver fittings, circa 1890. . . . . **£345**
British officer's white tropical helmet by Hawkes & Co., circa 1899 . . . . . . **£425**
Heavy cavalry helmet to the Somerset Yeomanry cavalry, circa 1845 to 1871. . . . . **£875**

Other ranks German helmet, Baden artillery dated 1916. . . . . **£300**

Reproduction Great Helm and Gauntlets. . . . **£125**

Leather tank helmet.
Warsaw Pact forces . . **£30**

Right:
British WWII helmet
with visor **£160**

WWII Russian
Front German cap
with earflaps
trimmed with
rabbit fur . . . **£125**

Bandsman's helmet
of the Cardigan
Royal Garrison
Volunteer Artillery
1902-1908 . . . . . . **£425**

A post 1902 officer's helmet of the Royal Horse Guards, silver plated skull, gilt mounts, velvet backed chinscales with ear rosettes, scarlet hair plume with large rosette, with a leather cover marked "RHG, Mounted Squadron Store" **£1,500**
A rare Victorian officer's helmet, worn 1853-55 of the Kent Artillery Militia, black PL skull with silver plated front peak binding, top mount with ball, and rose ornamentated plume socket, velvet backed chinscales and ear rosettes bearing Royal Crest, silver plated crowned escutcheon and wreath HP bearing gilt grenade over crossed cannon, at the foot a scroll "Kent", padded silk lining. Basically good condition, some service wear, grenade and lower left leaves of HP wreath loose, and cross missing from orb of crown, no plume **£850**

WWII Luftschutz helmet, Air Defence **£175**

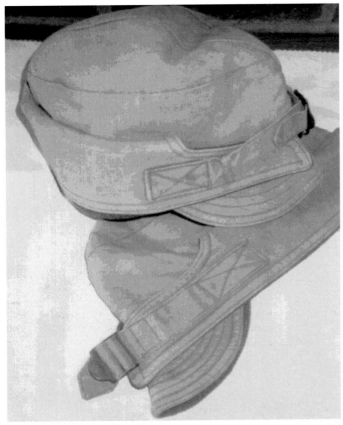

American ski caps, or cold weather headgear, Mark II, pre-1945 . . . . **£10**

Persian shield, circa 1800, chiselled steel with gold and silver decorations . . **£800**
Persian helmet, circa 1800, iron with gold and silver decoration,
and original camail **£800**

Spanish civil beret. Used by "Legion Condor" . . . . **PTS 150.000**

Tips for collectors

The pickelhaube was first introduced to the Prussian army in October 1842 to replace the bell-topped shako worn earlier. It was later adopted by Oldenburg – 1843; Hessen-Kassel – 1846; Baden – 1849; Hanover – 1849; Hesse-Darmstadt – 1849; Saxony – 1867; Wurttemberg – 1871; Bavaria – 1886; Brunswick – 1886. Variants were worn by the armed forces of other countries including: Sweden – 1845; Norway – 1845; Russia – 1846; Moldavia (Romania) – 1847; Denmark – 1851; Spain – 1855; England – 1878; USA – 1881; Portugal – 1885; Brazil – 1889; Chile – 1890; Argentina – 1900; Mexico – 1910.

Jaeger Shako in felt, for the German state of Meklenburg, dated 1916 . . . . . **£250**

THE GERMAN
M1916 PATTERN HELMET

At the beginning of WWI the German army was still equipped with the spiked leather helmet with metal fittings which had been standard issue in various forms since 1842. But times had changed and the nature of modern warfare now called for greater protection.

In 1915 a forward thinking Lieutenant Colonel serving in the mountainous Vosges region was instrumental in the development of a steel helmet which became known as the Gaede helmet (after the army group). As only about 1500 were made, these Gaede helmets with their distinctive nose protector, are now extremely rare.

The steel helmet proper came into being as a result of discussions between a neuro-surgeon who was having to deal with an influx of brain injuries as a result of shell fragments, and a technical expert. Dr. August Bier called for a strong yet light helmet to protect against the small shell fragments which were causing crippling brain damage in so many cases. Within weeks the development of the German steel helmet was begun.

Early specifications stated that the weight was not to exceed 1 kilo and that protection for the neck and forehead must be provided. By November 1915 the prototypes were being rigorously tested including being blasted by shrapnel shells fired from 10.5cm howitzers. With Teutonic thoroughness the helmets were examined in different heat conditions and with a variety of liners including rubber substitute, felt and horsehair, until the War Ministry was satisfied.

Finally the specifications for the first requisition of 30,000 helmets were agreed. The helmet was to be made of sheet steel from 1mm to 1.1mm in thickness, inwardly crimped around the rim and made so that the helmet stood roughly a two fingers

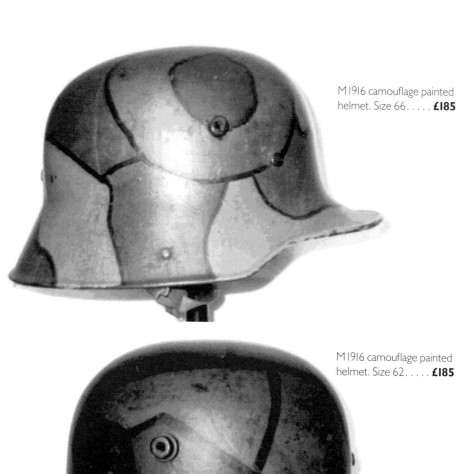

M1916 camouflage painted helmet. Size 66..... **£185**

M1916 camouflage painted helmet. Size 62..... **£185**

M1916 camouflage painted helmet. Size 64..... **£160**

span from the head. The liner was secured with three holes and on each side there was a hole for a ventilation lug and its retaining washer. The helmet dipped at the back to form a protective apron over the neck.

The first shipment of helmets for tests in the field went to the 1st Assault Battalion in December 1915 and by February the following year they were extensively introduced, priority being given to men fighting at Verdun and on the Somme.

Helmets were issued in six sizes (60, 62, 64, 66, 68, 70) and the size was stamped into the left inner side of the neck apron.

Various modifications were made over the years: for example, the demands of winter warfare called for the introduction of a white helmet cover and in 1917, due to a shortage of leather, the liner was modified by the replacement of the leather band which secured the liner pads with a sheet metal band.

Today German steel helmets of both world wars are amongst the most collected of items and prices range from the sublime to the ridiculous according to the rarity and condition of the helmet.

It should be noted that the prices shown alongside these models are purely a guide and it would be advisable to seek a qualified opinion on price if you wish to sell a particular helmet as condition and type affect the price so much.

FURTHER READING:
Ludwig Baer, The History of the German Steel Helmet 1916-1945
R. James Bender.

M1916 camouflage painted helmet. Size 66 with contemporary splinter damage **£160**

A very rare M1918 pattern 'trench special' helmet with non-reflective finish **£450**

M1916 camouflage painted helmet. Size 66 . . . . . **£185**

M1916 helmet with medics insignia to front. Size 62 . . . . **£160**

Above left: M1916 pattern helmet with late war 'splash' camouflage. Size 64. . . . . **£145**

Above: M1916 pattern helmet in exceptional condition. Size 64 . . . . **£135**

Left: M1918 helmet, insignia worn only by the 1st Foot Guards and the Guards Signal Battalion . . **£500 - £600**

Above: M1918 pattern helmet. Note the lack of rivets to lower skirt **£125**

Left: M1918 helmet with 'war splash' camouflage painted finish. Size 66 . . . . **£145**

UNIFORMS

Unlike some aspects of militaria, there is something about clothing that always remains personal to the wearer. A First World War hero's group of medals might be a tribute to his courage and a good financial investment, but the crumpled battledress in which he won his VC – that tells its own story of the hardship and squalor of the trenches and the blood and sweat of battle.

The move towards uniformly equipped forces was first made by the New Model Army of the English Civil War and later developed for the standing army after the Restoration of Charles II in 1660. Prior to that the fighting man's apparel was largely his own affair and distinguishing friend from foe on the battlefield often depended on luck and the wearing of some recognition mark – like an oak leaf twig.

Red has been a military colour for centuries because red cloth was inexpensive and today's ceremonial red tunic of the British Army is still as popular with collectors as the many variations which have arisen throughout the centuries. Examples of current ceremonial wear can be bought for a few pounds from a surplus dealer while serious collectors can pay hundreds of times that amount for a Georgian example.

What distinguishes most 18th- and 19th- century uniforms is their sheer impracticability for campaigning. Frock coats which impeded progress, tightly fitting jackets, enormous epaulettes, gold and silver lace and a colour that was easily distinguished through the smoke of a battlefield – the soldier of years gone by had much to contend with. Bearing in mind that much of the active service seen by the British Army was in the warmer parts of the Empire, some of the garments now treasured by collectors must have been torture to wear.

In general, it is the 'best' uniform which has survived, perhaps the one worn on special occasions or when the soldier returned home. It might have been packed away in a suitcase and forgotten about while the everyday uniform was consigned to a bonfire! So good original 'battle' or service dress from any period is highly prized and commands good prices, especially if it comes with some provenance. An officer's service dress tunic from the Second World War may be worth very little but his battledress tunic would be collectable.

Twentieth-century tunics are sometimes collected for the insignia that they carry. The value of Second World War British battledress can easily be exceeded by the value of the insignia associated with it.

Second World War Allied paratroop items and all kinds of German Third Reich uniforms are particularly sought after today and prices reflect this popularity.

Uniform collectors, like connoisseurs of wine, develop a 'nose' for the smell and texture of the fabric. Old wool, such as that found on 18th- and 19th-century tunics, has a characteristic smell, and the weight and drape of the garment all provide information to the expert. There is no substitute for experience here and the collector is advised to handle as many garments as possible, and to talk to other collectors and dealers to build up this intuitive skill.

Uniforms can be collected as representing a particular period, by regiment or arm of service, by war, by nationality – there are many variations – and most can be found at militaria fairs and shows. The following photographs give some examples of the variety available and prices that they are currently commanding.

Dispatch rider's trousers WWII dated............**£15**
A French cavalry tunic **£75**
WWII Officer's jacket...................................**£32**

This is one of the last tunics in 1945. Issued to a German Naval Coastal Artillery Sergeant......**£195**

A tunic of the 2nd Northumberland Volunteer Artillery – late Victorian ....**NPA**

Staffordshire Yeomanry Officer's epaulettes circa 1840, in their original metal box **£225**

Tunic to Lt. Col. of German Mountain troops. Edelweiss sleeve badge, regimental number to shoulder board **£395**
British Paratrooper's helmet, dated 1944......**£170**
2nd pattern smock battledress **£150**
1st type U.S. Navy fighter pilot's helmet **£250**

2 U.S. jackets: Captain Special Forces from the Green Berets **£40**
WWII 101st Airborne Division jacket............**£145**

Military Sporrans WWII vintage:
Gordon Highlander **£100**
Royal Scots...**£100**
Argyll & Sutherland Highlanders (swinging six)..**£120**
Glengarry: Argyll & Sutherland Highlanders **£75**
Kilt: box pleated,
Argyll and Sutherland Highlanders.................**£75**

RAF Tornado Pilot's equipment
Helmet, MK10B Life Preserver, speed jeans (anti-G-Garment, lower torso) ....**NPA**

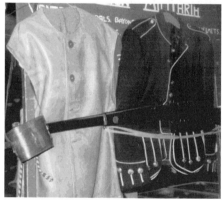

WWII leather jerkin **£35**
Scottish tunic..**£20**
P14 rifle and bayonet as used by the
Home Guard..**£165**

British desert camouflage jackets **£12**
Swiss camouflage suit...................................**£35**
Reproduction S.S.
WWII reversible smock...............................**£150**

A very rare 1918 pattern 'Russian blue' RAF jacket and trousers. (This pattern was only in use for 3 months)....................................**NPA**

A framed set of Para insignia. Their owner served between 1979 – 1994. Full history supplied ...**£50**

A complete uniform of the 101st Airborne – issued to a U.S. Colonel. Dates from Mid 60's. With WWII and Vietnam medal ribbons, 1st class combat clasp, infantry insignia and parachute jump wings and silver colonel shoulder eagles.........**£90**

Waffen S.S. "Handschar" division NCO's tunic circa 1943...**£1250**

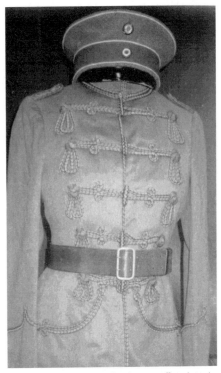

Extremely rare German line hussar officer's tunic, cap, breeches and belt circa 1914.................**£950**

Luftwaffe WWII officer's Fliegerblouse.........**£450**

Swiss camouflage suit complete **£30**
FAL SLR (deactivated)................................**£190**

Russian airforce Colonel's jacket (new) **£50**
Russian army Colonel's jacket with badge of Russian military forces (new) **£45**

Full dress uniform to Captain in the Grenadier Guards (with bearskin)...............................**£800**

FURTHER READING

Andrew Mollo, Uniforms of the S.S. (collected edition) – Windrow & Green

---

Shell jacket (officer's) 66th Berkshire Regt ...**£245**

WWII Leather Flying Jacket of the 14th Army Air Force (the Flying Tigers) – includes a large cloth 14th AF roundel to right chest, another silver embroidered tiger patch to left chest, silver embroidered China-Burma-India Command flash to left shoulder, on the back a linen "Blood Chit" with Chinese inscription offering a reward to anyone helping the wearer to return to base if shot down over enemy territory, various stamps including "1941" and "Flying Tiger".............**£360**
Painted jacket to the 14th AF, roundel to left chest, with name tag "CD Moizahn" above, gilt embroidered roundel to right shoulder, stencilled leather China-Burma-India Command flash to left shoulder, silk "Blood Chit" on back **£310**

S.S. NCO's service tunic, BW markings. Iron Cross 2nd class, combat award for bravery, Russian campaign medal for the Winter War 1941-42, war merit medal with swords 2nd class (for war effort) S.S. flashes, collar badges. Combat tunic made into a walking out tunic **£900**
Nazi street flag.............**£120**

Lieutenant Herman Goring Division fliegerblouse **£385**

U.S. EM 1939 service coat, Ordnance **£52**
U.S. EM 1939 service coat, 5th Airforce **£47**
U.S. WWII officer's "Chocolate" service coat to the Army Air Corps **£52**

Captain's tunic to the Queens Royal Irish Hussars, dated March 1961 ....**£25**

Police riot equipment including 7.62mm bullet proof vest **£110**
Fire retardant overalls **£25**
Leg and shin protectors **£25**
Gloves **£10**
Helmet.............**£30**

S.S. man's herringbone tunic with engineer's epaulettes circa 1943 ....**£675**

U.S. officer's tunic and pinks to a 2nd Lt. 505 TL Parachute Infantry 82nd Airborne, with sterling silver jump wings and C.I.B., Silver Star, Bronze Star & Purple Heart. Dated 1943 ....**£215**

Victorian 1881 pattern staff sergeant's jacket to the 1st Volunteer Battalion East Lancs Regt **£95**

Third Reich naval petty officer's mess jacket dated 9th December 1935 .....**£250**

Victorian 1881 pattern Artillery Patrol Jacket to a major. Complete with a false collar **£95**

Tips for collectors

In November 1944 collar-attached shirts, for wear with a tie were introduced for use by Other Ranks of the British Army. This resulted in the increased wearing of battledress blouses with the collar open, exposing shirt and tie – previously only the prerogative of officers. From this date many soldiers had their blouses modified by having the now exposed lapels faced in a material other than the drill fabric with which they were lined on issue.

Swiss Alpine cammo uniform, helmet cover, back-pack, trousers, complete **£30**

British WWII Battledress Blouses:
RASC £45
REME £45
79th Armoured Division
(plastic officer's rank) £35

German officer's hat, jacket, epaulettes, Iron
Cross and medal ribbons $1,000

Irish Guards Drummer's tunic, post 1952.......£85

Soviet Admiral's tunic, trousers and cap £275

Honourable Artillery Company tunic and busby
dated 1909 ....£350

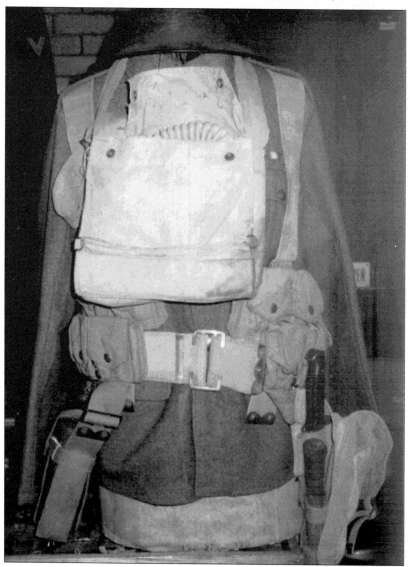

WW1 other ranks tunic and accoutrements, including 1908 pattern webbing straps, water bottle,
belt, bayonet, brodie helmet and small box respirator – all in good condition
NPA

Tips for collectors

To test whether a uniform has had cloth insignia stitched on at a later date try the thread test. Modern threads are usually synthetic, whereas those of 50 or more years ago were made from natural fibres such as cotton. Take a sample of thread, expose it to heat (a match flame, for example) and watch the results. Polyester thread, unlike cotton, melts before burning, then burns vigorously and brightly with the distinctive smell of burning plastic. It leaves a sooty residue whereas cotton leaves a greyish-white ash.

Luftwaffe Fliegerblouse, flight section jacket dated 1939 ....**£280**

Captain's jacket to the East Hampton division of the New York City fire department, including cap, trousers and badges **£100**

Left: 1940 Austerity pattern battledress blouse issued in 1944, it has converted lapels and was issued to a 2nd Lieutenant in the Buffs Control Commission in Germany **£45**

Above:
Dorset Regt mess waist-coat, late Victorian **£35**
Dorset Regt Officer's patrol jacket 1890's. ...**£90**

Left to right: Saxon parade tunic to the 12th Grenadiers 1910-1918 ....**£265**
German WWII dress tunic 117th Infantry **£365**
Bavarian musician's tunic early 1900's **£260**

German Nazi Order Police tunic to a senior NCO, including cap.....................................**£275**
Original Russian Boudionovka cap from Russian-Finish war of 1939-40 ....**£75**
Two medals and death plaque **£45**

Scottish style doublet fronted tunic to a Lt. Colonel of the Glasgow Highlanders. Dated February 1918. Ribbons for 1914/18 Victory and war medal, 1914/18 Territorial force medal, Territorial Efficiency medal, military long service medal. Two years overseas service chevrons on sleeve. . **£120**

FURTHER READING
British Army Uniforms & Insignia of World War Two. *Brian L. Davis.*
Arms & Armour Press

Ceremonial home dress uniform to a corporal in the Royal Air Force Central Band, complete with trousers, busby and tunic, aiguillettes and shoulder knots. **£185**

Tunic. Edward VII period. Retains part of its original paper label. (without the belt). **£85**

FURTHER READING

The Scottish Soldier
Stephen Wood. Archive Publications Ltd.

Warwickshire Regiment Tunic, signaller badges, and other badges on sleeve. Thought to be late WWI. **£150**

WWII Wehrmacht tan water camouflage winter jacket . . . **£295** Waffen S.S. camouflage reversible winter jacket . . . . **£850** Wehrmacht 2nd model camouflage smock **£650**

Cuirass breastplate as worn by Samurai Warriors during the EDO period 1600-1870 . . . . **NPA**

Cromwellian period pikeman's armour, circa 1640 . . . . **£4,750**

Left: Army Medical Reserve Hauptmann Parade Jacket, hat and trousers and awards. Condition near mint – all clothing named to the same man . . . . **US $1,900**

Below: Buckskin jacket . . . . **US $3,500**
Armour . . . . **US $160 – $2,500**

Panzer denim wrapover jacket WWII dated £185

Reproduction Roman Segmentata Lorika £180
Roman Helmet £165

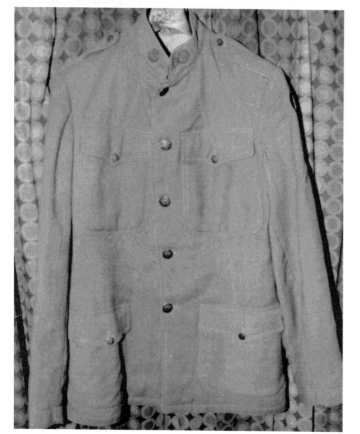

WW1 U.S. Tunic with all original badges. £75

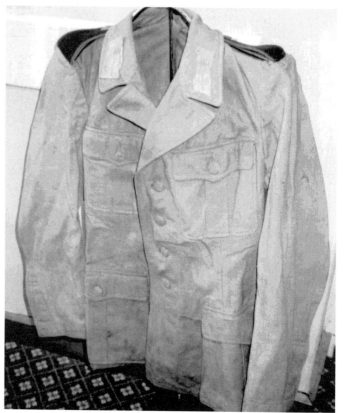

German Afrika Korps tunic, dated 1942, with collar patches and shoulder
straps. This type of tunic was re-issued to the Czech Army and is date
stamped 1946, about the time the Czech Republic was formed £275

S.S. Herringbone fatigue tunic, fully marked circa 1938 . . . . **£275**

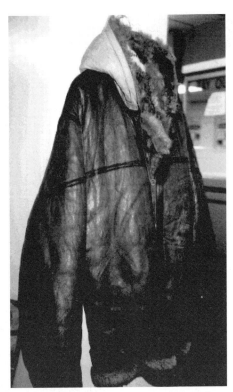

Unusual flying jacket with hood in leather and sheepskin, for Coastal Command and the Atlantic. Dated 1943 . . . . **NPA**

WWII German motor cycle coat in rubberised fabric. **£350**

Los Angeles Police Department
SWAT Uniform **£65**
Night stick. **£35**

German jacket and hat to Lieutenant in the Pioneers with badges, awards etc.
Hat included . . . . **US $1,200**

U.S. Army/Airforce tunic, 1942 dated to a Technical Sergeant of the 3rd Air Force. Previously belonged to 15th Air Force. Honourable discharge badge (ruptured duck) branch of service badge. Medal ribbons: European theatre, good conduct, Purple Heart. Plus garrison cap with Air Force piping. **£65**

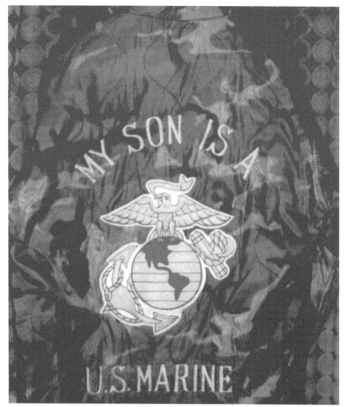

U.S. Women's 'Tour Jacket' **£35**

American WWI Doughboy jacket to the 12th Division, large size with overseas chevrons and all brass collar discs etc. Complete . . . . **US $375**

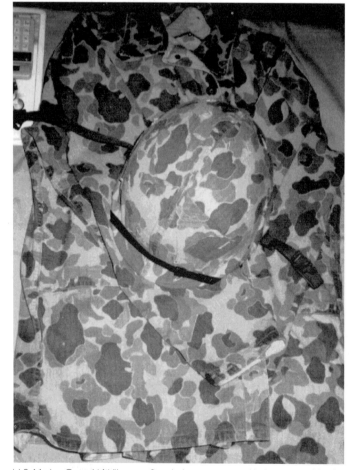

U.S. Marine Corps WWII camouflage jacket, trousers and helmet cover. Used principally in the Pacific, it is reversible to autumn brown. In Europe it was too easily confused with S.S. reversible to be safe for wearer. Set . . . . **US $875**

Edwardian Lifeguard Trooper's helmet and Cuirass **£1,250**

Russian cold weather jacket, dated 1980. Fake fur collar and padded lining **£25**

Two suits of armour in excellent condition, Victorian manufacture (each) **£1,270**

Pompiers jacket 1860 and giberne . . . . . . **600 FF**

Royal Naval Division tunic, helmet and documents. Named and dated WWI **£550**

Scaled down 24" high model of English Armour **£325**

German Wehrmacht cadet tunic 1936. No Waffenfarbe on shoulder boards because the wearer had not yet specialised **£295**

Cuirassie la Garde 1854 . . . . **9,500 FF**
Infantry Shako 2nd Empire 1860 . . . . . . **2,500 FF**

EQUIPMENT

As well as his uniform and weapon, the soldier down the ages has been equipped with a vast amount of material to support life in camp and on campaign. From boot cleaning equipment to a 'housewife' to enable him to make uniform repairs, mess tin to field dressing, entrenching tool to field telephone, all this and much more has resulted in plenty of choice for the collector or re-enactor.

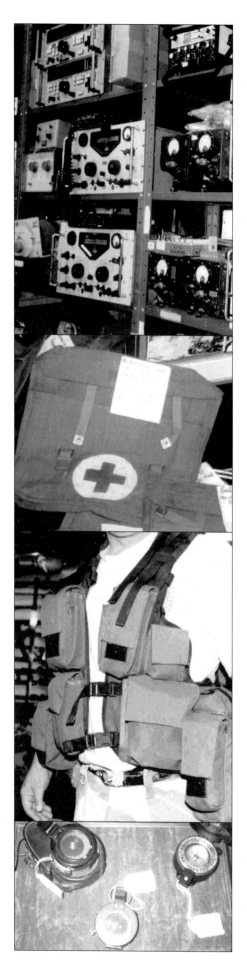

Some of the private purchase items deemed necessary for the gentleman soldier campaigning in India or Africa, such as a portable shower bath or a mahogany recumbent easy chair with reading board, are unlikely to turn up at the average military fair, and infrequently at auction. However, collectors can choose from a wide array of more modern items of equipment.

Aviation instruments are particularly popular and specialist aero-jumble events are devoted to this collecting interest. Bits and pieces from wrecked aircraft or mounted souvenirs from shot down planes can be found along with a huge variety of aircrew equipment – masks, radios, chronometers and so on. Battle of Britain souvenirs are particularly sought after.

Naval enthusiasts can acquire high-quality precision instruments such as German U-boat binoculars, sextants and compasses, if they are prepared to pay the prices which these very collectable items command.

From an earlier era powder flasks are frequently seen and brass, pewter and horn examples can be bought at moderate cost.

Diligent searching at militaria events should reward ordnance enthusiasts with such equipment as clinometers, fuse setters or gun directors, whilst military vehicle owners striving for authenticity can pick up all sorts of WW2 items at moderate cost.

The system for disposal of UK Government surplus has changed in the last two years; much more is being exported which is gradually having an impact on the surplus and collecting market. Surplus dealers in the UK now import more European equipment than previously which adds to the range seen at militaria fairs. The modern surplus/ collectable market still depends to a large extent on the 'newsworthiness' of various conflicts as equipment and uniforms seen on television become more desirable to the collector. Much of this surplus equipment, manufactured to very high standards, sells for just a few pounds.

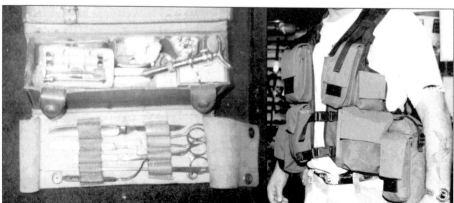

A selection of original Nazi MG34 spares.
Magazine drum WW2 . . . . **£20**
Nazi drill rounds **£6**
MG13/34 anti-aircraft goggles **£12**
MG34 double magazine drum with carrier. **£65**

Panzer MG34s. **DM700**
MG42 – dug up restored **DM500**
MG34 de-activated **DM500**

Two U.S. field telephones and a half mile of cable, Vietnam era **£45**

German propaganda radio with WW2 bakelite case and eagle/swastika
emblem on front . . . . **NPA**
British goggles WW2. . . . . **£15**
British oxygen mask WW2 . . . . **£25**
Toy British searchlight made in 1940s. **£15**

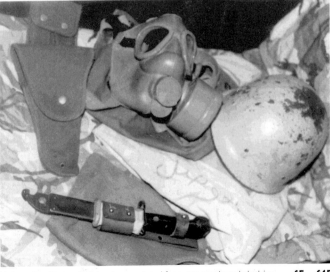

Various Iraqi items, holster, bayonet and frog, gas mask and clothing . . . **£5 – £45**

WWI trench lamp in original leather case, named to Captain W. P. Lousada of the Norfolk Regiment. **£95**

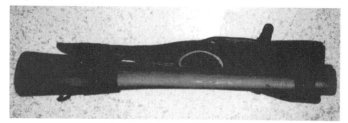

U.S. Army pick and mattocks in canvas carrying pouch dated 1944 . . **US $40**

Kriegsmarine sextant by C. Plath, Hamburg . . . . **2,500 FF**

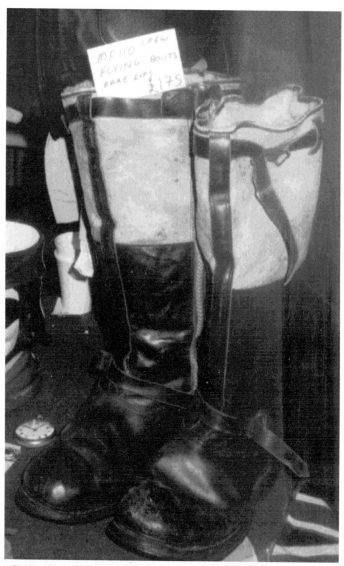

ME110 flying crew boots with rare zips **£175**

R.R.C. six transceiver field radios. **£45**

Naval rangefinder in case (for keeping station in a convoy) **£55**

Hundreds of pairs of boots.
Genuine Army ski boots **£20**
Assorted Army boots . . . . **£4.95 – £45**

Baigisch 7C night vision binocular 2 + generation **£820**

British WW2 mountaineering boots worn by Artillery Officer in the Italian
campaign **£45**

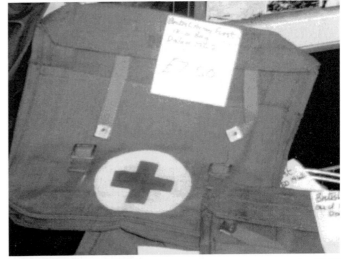

British Army First Aid bags 1942 . . . . **£7.50**

Two holsters, circa 1960 officer's "Guardia de Franco"
Left: . . . . **PTS 60.000**
Right: . . . . **PTS 75.000**

WW2 marching compass 1943 . . . . **£95**
WWI prismatic compass issued to officer complete with leather carrying
case. Issued to a Lieutenant in the South Staffs Regiment, dated 1916. . . **£125**

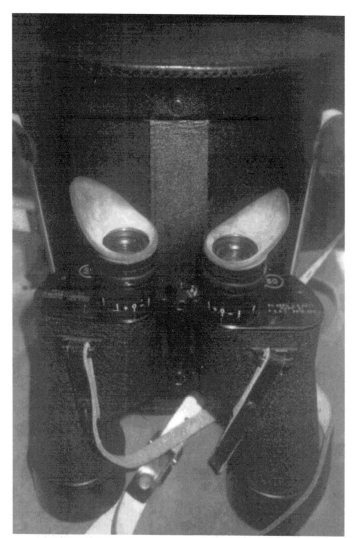

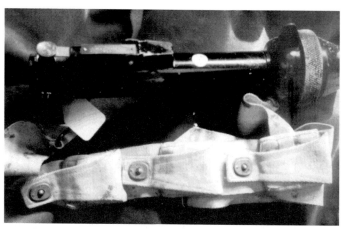

WW2 Naval commando signal torch with Morse key and filters in canvas sling pouches . . . . **NPA**

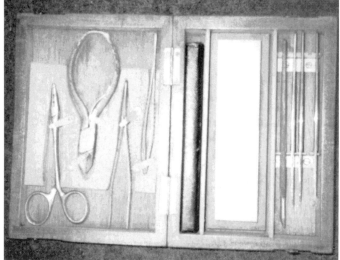

U.S. Naval binoculars 7 x 50 magnification in leather case. Current issue **£80**

WWI Field surgeon's kit in mahogany fitted case. **£120**

Ammunition boxes . . . . **£1.50 – £5.90**

British Naval ship's compass, circa 1900 with paraffin lamp at side **£350**

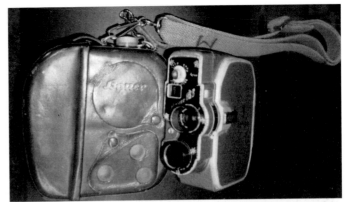

Kriegsmarine movie camera 1939 . . . . **£300**

Russian bakelite cased field telephone from the cold war period **£25**

Racal RA17 radio receivers, fully refurbished and aligned **£200**

Officer's waist belt clasp 1881-1944 in silver and gilt **£80**

Belts, top to bottom:
WWI Imperial German Army belt, leather, with steel buckle **£60**
WWI Imperial German Army belt, leather with brass buckle **£50**
Telegraph troops belt, leather with steel buckle. WWI, very rare **£150**
WWI officer's dress belt, metallic woven fabric **£95**

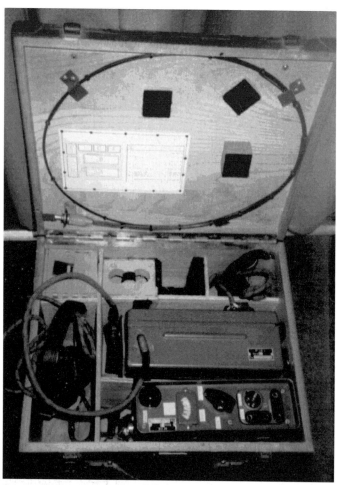

Czech radio in wooden case. Army issue **£160**

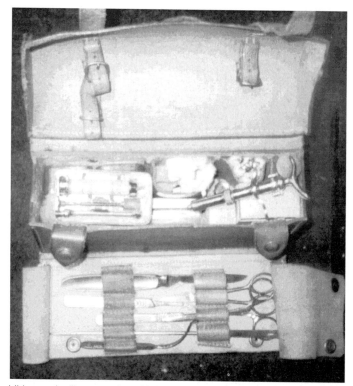

Hide cased military veterinary kit. War Dept marked, dated 1944 . . . . . **£200**

WWII Nazi bunker
lantern. **£35**

Flying helmet. **£75**
RAF flying overalls. **£30**
German parachute **£48**
Drogue parachute for cargo **£17**
RAF type SS Mk15 life raft. **£65**

Iraqi gas mask from the Gulf War **£12**
Red Cross mug **£2.50**
WW2 Lamp **£6**

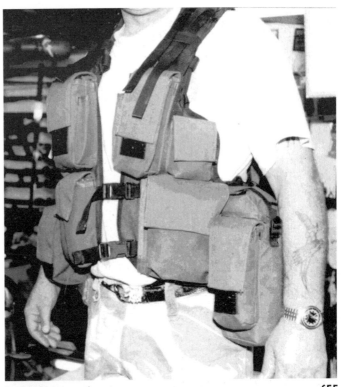

South African assault vest **£55**

Lizars of Glasgow & Edinburgh deer scope with leather case,
extends to 2'6" **£195**

Early German leather belt with all brass S.A. buckle, circa 1935 .... **£70**

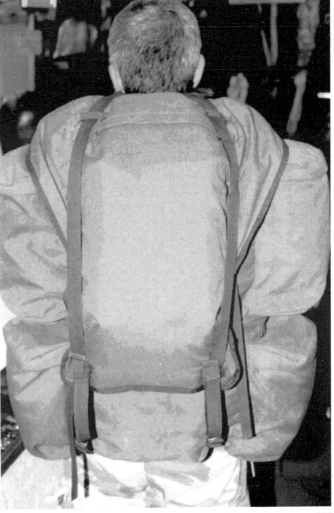

South African bergen **£50**

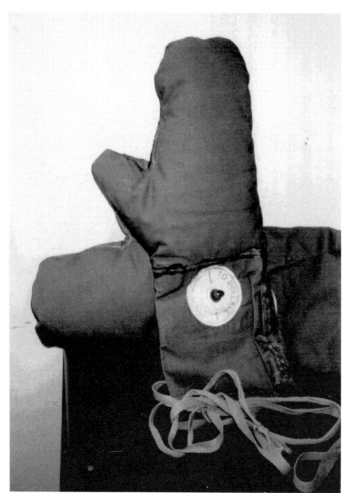

British Tx, Rx radio **£75**
U.S. PRC Six radio **£50**

Royal Navy inflatable cold weather gloves from the 1950s. **£12**

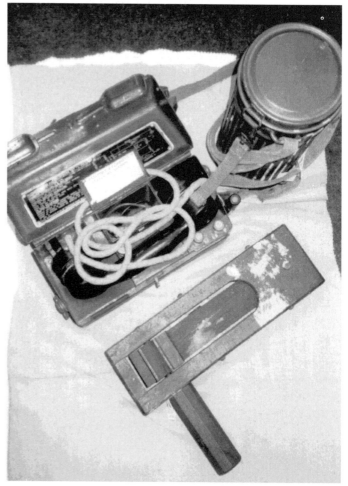

American shovel cover WW2 . . . . **£3.50**
U.S. Marine Corps wire cutter pouch WWI **£15**
American Air Force first aid kit **£16**
WW2 "Woodsman's pal" U.S. Navy issue. Includes sharpening stone and
booklet, unissued and unused **£180**

British WW2 field telephone in metal case **£10**
German gas mask, post WW2 . . . . **£20**
British WW2 Home Guard standard issue gas rattle **£10**

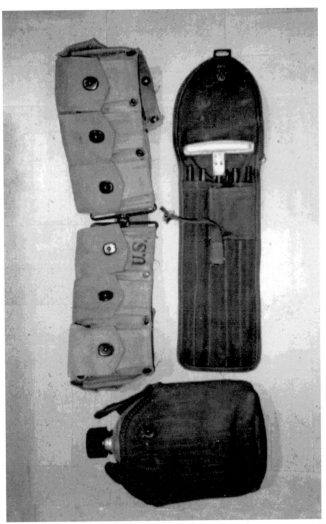

British 1939-45 pattern army gas mask **£12**

U.S. water bottle, Korean War. **£15**
U.S. Garand ammunition belt. **£15**
U.S. .50 cal machine gun cleaning kit. WW2 . . . . **£20**

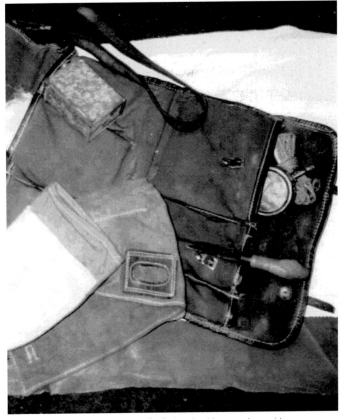

WW2 American tanker's helmet, with leather lining. Made by Spalding . . . **£150**

Post WW2 Eastern European MG 42 cleaning kit, complete with canvas
receiver cover, barrel changing mitt, oil cans and tools **£55**

Rare 1857 Hardings patent holster, with japanned magazine, for combustible cartridge and percussion caps. Brass plate embossed "Deane & Sons King William St., London Bridge" **£330**

WWI wash kit roll, containing economy fibre button stick, toothbrush, razor blades, shaving soap stick, spoon, fork and other sundry items, such as toilet paper, spare boot laces, eating knife and soap **£18**
Drinking mug, war time pattern, brown enamel, I pint **£5**
Soap **£8**
Hairbrush **£5**
Dark green webbing blanco **£5**

WWI 50 round bandolier, dated 1915, used by mounted troops, (Non-cavalry) **£25**

WW2 felt covered water bottle and webbing carrier. Bottle **£5**
Carrier **£3.50**

WW2 Nazi M.G. 34 tin, with lots of spares **£45**

WWI German ammunition pouches, dated 1914 . . . . **£15**

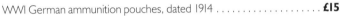

WWI leather Sam Browne dress belt. **£18**

WW2 Brown leather A.T.S. boots on left **£55**
Top: Black Canadian "Ammo" boots, so called because this type of boot is believed to have been issued under the stores reference as "Boots Ammunition" **£35**
Below: WW2 A.T.S. brown leather standard walking-out shoes **£40**
Anti-gas dubbin, protection for leather boots and shoes. Tin. **£7**
Genuine "Wrens" WW2 shoe polish. Tin. **£8**
Foot powder (talcum powder) to keep feet dry and to prevent
"Trench Foot". Tin **£7.50**

WW2 Russian army officer's belt. . . . . **400,000 roubles**

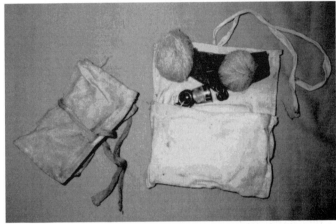

WW2 "Housewife" containing needles, darning wool, thimble, spare shirt and battledress buttons. **£10**

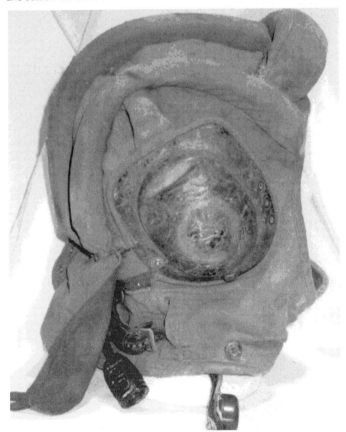

WW2 Russian tank helmet, with captured German electric loom. . . . . . . **NPA**

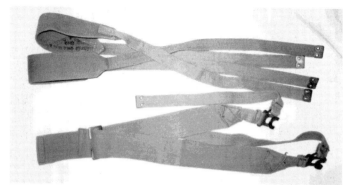

WW2 37 pattern webbing equipment shoulder straps **£2.50**
Pack strap for attaching pack to straps, commonly known as "L" straps . **£3.50**

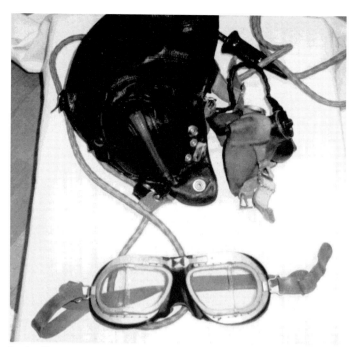

Battle of Britain pilot's leather flying helmet,
with goggles and oxygen mask **£275**

1917 German leather Luger holster, officer issue **£75**

Boer War leather .303 bandolier with brass hangers,
for use with the British cavalry **£25**

WWII officer's trench lamp
with red and green sliding filters.
Would work with a bicycle
torch battery. It still has its
original spare bulb. **£15**

WWI mounted troops water bottle and felt carrier with leather straps . . **£35**

U.S. Naval binoculars with case, missing straps, in used condition, 7 x 50 magnification, made by National Instruments, Houston TX in the mid 40s . . . . **US $150**

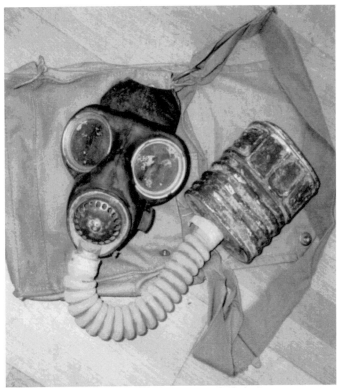

WW2 French resistance helmet with leather liner, and rayon armband . . **£40**
WW2 French army issue water bottle **£20**

WW2 British infantry pattern gas mask in canvas case. **£16**

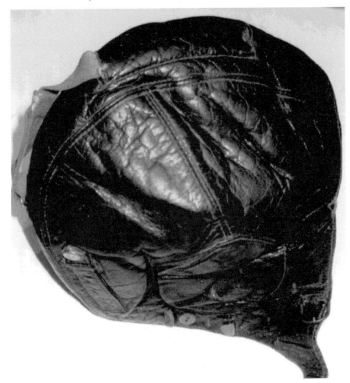

WW2 Leather, sheepskin lined Luftwaffe flying helmet, dated 1943 . . . . **£150**

U.S. Army field stove, complete and in working order. Original tags and instructions still legible, dated 1945 . . . . **US $75**

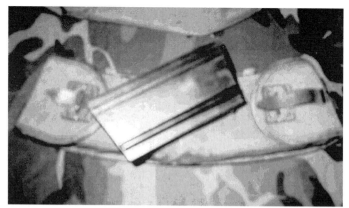

Waffen stamped MG 13 carrier and ammo clips (4) condition near mint.
Dated 1935 . . . . **US $75**

U.S. Civil War cross belt bullet pouch by L. Head & Co. Quincy, Illinois. With
original interior metal bullet tray **£325**

Nazi MG 34 drum magazine, with links and starter tab **£20**

Swiss bandolier WW2. . . . . **£18**

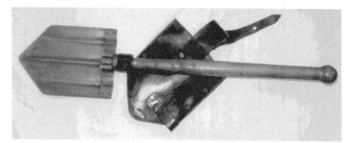

German WW2 entrenching tool, dated 1940, with leather holder **£130**

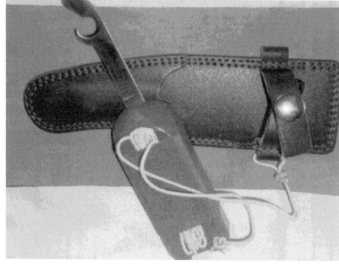

R.A.F. dinghy knife for use in a life raft. Date unknown, current style **£10**

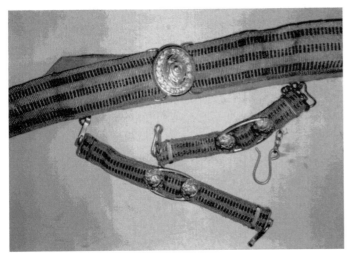

Soviet Naval officer's parade belt and dagger hangers, circa 1960s. Woven in metallic thread. **£40**

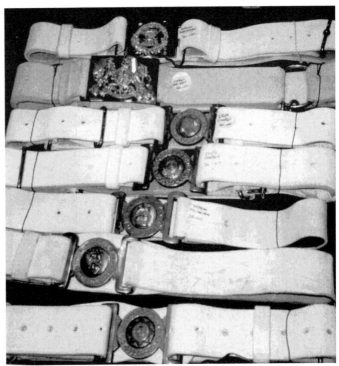

Belts, from the Victorian period to the present day, top to bottom:
Gordon Highlanders **£30**
Life Guards (dress belt) **£40**
Irish Guards **£30**
Scots Guards. **£30**
Victorian Volunteers **£35**
Edwardian general service **£30**
Coldstream Guards **£30**

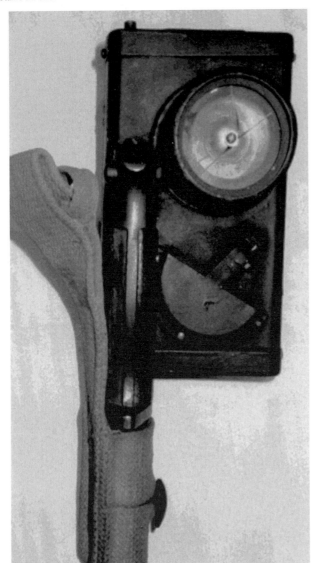

WWI signal lamp. Unusual because it attaches to 1907 bayonet. Has a removable top lid with extension lead inside. Normally has a red filter that is attached to a length of string, which enables a change of filter to give a danger signal. As shown in the photograph, it could be attached to the bayonet, enabling the soldier to stick it in the ground, so he could move away to a safer position **£65**

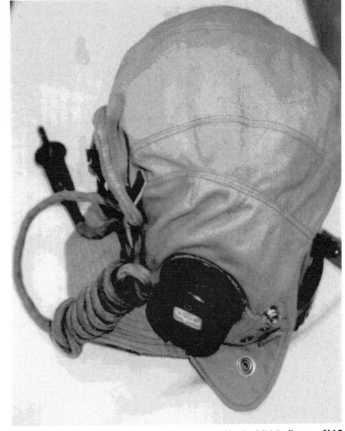

British WWII D. type canvas flying helmet, as used in the Middle East . . **£160**

MEDALS

From the Waterloo medal to the German Iron Cross, with thousands of variations of campaign, gallantry and commemorative medals in between, collectors today are assured of ample choice as well as a sound investment. The medal market continues to show growth and the pastime is as popular as ever. Although medal dealers are represented at almost all general militaria collectors' events, there are also specialist medal fairs and enthusiasts usually subscribe to auction houses and leading medal dealers for regular sales lists.

Apart from gallantry awards such as the Victoria Cross which are beyond the reach of most collectors, at the more expensive end of the UK market, the Napoleonic Wars' Naval and Military General Service medals are keenly collected and fetch high prices. Victorian campaign medals, especially pre-Crimean and Zulu War are also in great demand. Here the combination of bars and, above all, the story attached to the medal or group is all-important. Medals with paperwork and perhaps a photograph, which have been researched and offer the possibility of further investigation, are the favourites.

Pip, Squeak and Wilfred – the three First World War medals – can be relatively inexpensive but offer the possibility of interesting research. Again those belonging to casualties or whose medals are part of a gallantry group are most expensive, as are those to 'good' regiments such as the Guards. By contrast, the Second World War is a relatively lean period for medal enthusiasts as most of the campaign medals issued with some exceptions, were unnamed and therefore impossible to authenticate or research if separated from any provenance.

For those seeking something a little out of the ordinary, there is a multitude of colourful world orders and decorations available as well as miniature replicas which are worth considering if the budget does not run to the real thing.

The German Iron Cross, dating from 1813, and covering the First World War is one of the most distinctive pieces on the market. Around three quarters of a million were issued for Imperial German service and the award was revived by Hitler and issued in various divisions, for example, First and Second Class, Knight's Cross etc. Here, as in many aspects of Third Reich militaria, reproductions abound and have been known to fool the expert as well as the amateur. As one leading Third Reich dealer put it: "These things were being faked before the ink was dry on the treaty..." That being the case, the Latin tag 'caveat emptor' was never more apt.

FURTHER READING:
Robert W Gould. British Campaign Medals – Waterloo to the Gulf.
Arms and Armour Press

E.C. Joslin, A.R. Litherland and B.T. Simpkin.
British Battles and Medals. Published by Spinks

DCM George VI first type. In original presentation card box dated 1944. DCM immediate award 17th March 1944 with letter from Irish Guards RHQ stating "he was shot in the shoulder whilst holding off a German attack to enable his Company to retire, in Italy, and became a prisoner of War **£1,750**

WWI medals to Lieutenant Colonel T. A. Higginbottom RFA Mid 18.5.17 plus DSO. Victory Medal Renamed . . . . **NPA**

A Crimean Distinguished Medal Group, with French Legion of Honour, to the 39th Regiment with extensive research and photograph included. Below: Single medals from . . . . **£155 – 245**

Saudi Arabian Liberation of Kuwait Medal. . . . **£22**

Queen's Gallantry Medals. C.S.M. Northern Ireland. Gulf War Medal, L.S. & G.C. RUC. L.S. & G.C. All to a sergeant in the Intelligence Corps Queen's Gallantry Medal for undercover operations whilst attached to the RUC in Northern Ireland. Later attached to the S.A.S. in the Gulf War. **£7,500**

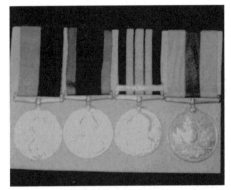

Medals to Sowar Jamal Khan 1st Bombay Lancers & Dist. D.C.O. Lancers **£335**

Russian Order of Glory, (awarded for courage) . . . . . **100,000 roubles**

Indian Order of Merit 2nd Class 1837-1912. Silver, gold & enamelled. Only 130 ever awarded. **£750**

Officer's Cross of War "Cristina" 1900-1931 . . . . (Spanish) **PTS 90.000**

Group to recipient who served on HMS Ajax against the Graf Spey 13th December 1939. . **£285**

WWI Watercolour with British War Medal and Victory Medal to Lieutenant Young of the Machine Gun Corps **£75**
From the same family, an extremely rare combination of Military Crosses and Military Medal and 14-15 Trio **£1,100**

British Orders including: Order of St. Michael & St. George neck badge **£345**
Order of Bath Knight Commander neck badge in silver, gilt and enamel **£550**
Knight's Batchelor badge in case of issue **£240**
The most excellent order of the Indian Empire Grand Commander's sash badge in gold and enamel, with full sash **£2,950**

A group of miniatures attributed to Vice Admiral M.R. Hill. R.N. In case. **£225**

A collection of medals to the Black Watch. D.S.O., Legion of Honour, Order of Crown of Belgium to Colonel S.H. Eden, mentioned in dispatches 6 times. **£2,000**
Pair and plaque to Charles Reid. Also D.C.M. plus others to his father **£850**

Genuine WWII stock Purple Heart with original suspender. Medal bar and miniature medal bar for civilian wear **£35**

Cased Orange order of Nassau.
Dutch, post WWII **£575**
French Legion of Honour. Pre-WWII **£175**
Order of Belgium Lion. Post WWII **£200**
Order of Social Merit. French Pre-WWII . . . **£130**
Order of St. Sava. Serbian. Pre-WWII **£160**

Waterloo period medals to the 11th Light Dragoons 1815. (This was the first war medal to be awarded to everyone who took part in the campaign and the first medal to be named to the men who qualified for it) **£425**
Naval group for the Baltic and Crimea campaign 1854-1856. . . . . **£175**

MBE DCM Group. WWI & WWII Medals. 2 Territorial Medals. French Medal Militaire to a Battery Sergeant, Warwickshire Garrison Artillery **£750**

Distinguished Flying Cross Group with Air Efficiency Award to a pilot who flew Halifax bombers against many heavily defended targets in Germany. Comes with his flying log book, photographs and original documents **£795**

DFC reverse engraved 1945, AFM, 1939-45 star, F&G star, Defence medal. With Postagram congratulating recipient of DFC in London Gazette 17th July 1945, and news cutting stating recipient received an AFC from the King with follow-up correction to AFC. **£1,100**

Steinhaur und Luck manufactured Knight's Cross of the Iron Cross **£2,650**

Early Indian Campaign Group, to the Bengal Artillery covering campaigns from 1842-1858 . . . . **£850**

Left: West Wall Medal, awarded initially for assisting in building of the Siegfried Line. Also given to people who served on the building and manning of the Atlantic Wall **£10**
Right: WWII German Russian Front Medal, for service in Russia 1941/42 . . . . **£18**

China Medal 1900 clasp, Relief of Peking. . . . **£148**
Indian Distinguished Service Medal **£205**
Victorian Long Service Good Conduct Medal to the 7th Dragoon Guards 1886 . . . . **£58**
Distinguished Conduct Medal to a Sgt. in the Royal Field Artillery 1917 . . . . **£295**
Cased Military Cross 1943 . . . . **£230**

Combat Service Medal
WWII onwards . . . . **50,000 roubles**
Bravery Medal, WWII onwards . . **75,000 roubles**

WWII German West Wall Medal, for helping to construct the Siegfried Line **£10**

WWI Military Medal and pair to the London Regiment, with cap badge. Private R.G. Stacy . . **£160**

A group awarded to Colonel James Dras Fulton D.S.O. M.C. with one of only nine Order of the Lion and Sun of Persia, awarded in the Great War 1914-18. Later being awarded one of the only four Distinguished Service Orders for Burma, 1930-32. . . . . **£2,995**

Soviet WWII set of all three Orders of Glory. There were only just over 2,000 recipients of all three classes, always awarded to non commissioned officers for hand to hand combat. These recipients are held in the same high esteem as Heroes of the Soviet Union. Includes an Award Book with photos which entitle the holder to special privileges. Also newspaper article giving details of his exploits, and photographs. Full documentation. **£2,250**

Top, left to right:
German WWII War Merit Cross 2nd Class, with swords (military) **£15**
German WWII War Merit Medal **£8**
Lower: German WWII War Merit Cross, (without swords) 2nd class (civilian) **£12**

Group of seven. Elizabeth II D.C.M. Group. To the 7th Gurkhas, awarded for the Malayan emergency in 1954. The recipient was wounded in action but personally killed two bandits. . **£5,000**
Albert Medal/Military Medal group to the 12th Lancers, both awarded for bravery in the 1914-18 war. **£6,000**

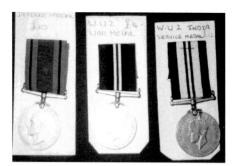

WWII British defence medal £10
WWII British war medal. £4
WWII India service medal £12

American Distinguished Flying Cross . . £18

Right: Order of the Red Banner. (Awarded for heroic deeds) 1928-1991) . . **150,000 roubles**

WWII British Stars:
Pacific star £20
Atlantic star £15
1939-45 star £15
Air crew Europe star (replacement) £9

Left: Current issue American Silver Star (for valour). £14
Right: American Legion of Merit (for valour) . £25

A Sudan 1896-89 group of medals awarded to W.O.I. W.T. Hooper, Army Service Corps. A rare group of medals to a British soldier who served, attached to the Egyptian Army. £425

The Most Excellent Order of the British Empire. Dames Commander's, (D.B.E.) neck and brass badge. King George and Queen Mary £480

Left: German veteran's medal. The 1914-18 cross of honour. Awarded to veterans in WWII for service in WWI £5

Framed group of medals and insignia to Lieutenant Colonel Francis Cecil Campbell Balfour, Northumberland Fusiliers. Grandson of the 8th Duke of Argyll – comes with complete history **£2,250**

Below left: Medal group (eleven in total) in glass case by Spinks 1950. To Colonel acting Brigadier General James Dees Fulton 2/15th Punjab Regiment. The Lion and Sun of Persia, extremely rare, only 9 awarded. D.S.O. is for Burma. One of only 4 awarded. Complete with all original bestowal for D.S.O. dated 20.12.32. Plus original commission dated 1908. Original D.I.D.'s (9 in total) from 1916 to 1935 . . . **£3,650**

EQUIPMENT

French WW2 waterbottle **£22**

British civilian WW2 gas mask in brass coloured tin box **£10**
WWII Mauser K98 cleaning kit **£6**
French WW1 hand grenade **£19**
Japanese 7.7mm rounds with original box **£25**

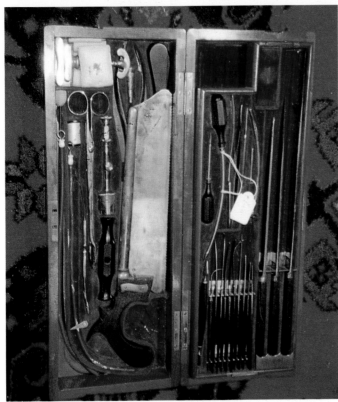

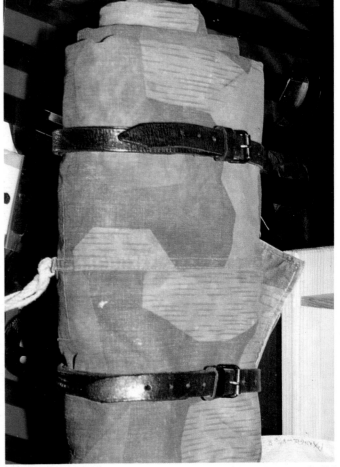

Cased field surgeon's medical kit. Totally complete with Liston knives,
bone saws, trepan (for drilling holes in the head), scalpels, probes,
cannulas, tourniquet, bullet remover, needles and thread.
Also included in this kit is a tracheotomy instrument, in silver to avoid
infection. All instruments have ebony handles and come in a mahogany case.
Dated between 1860 – 1880. . . . . **£1,875**

WW2 German standard issue Zeltbard with RB numbers. **£35**

An assortment of German WWI and WW2 medals, badges and regalia.
Prices from **£8**

French Legion of Honour. French Croix de Guerre, Member Victorian
Order, 1914-15 Trio to Rear Admiral Cunningham **£450**

British WW2 "stars" Left to right:

Burma Star **£15**
France and Germany Star **£12**
Africa Star **£5.50**
Italy Star **£6**

Indian Mutiny Medal 1857 to Jemadar Sowdagur 20th Regiment Punjab . **£80**
Shipwrecked fisherman and marines. Royal Benevolent Society. **£95**
Kandahar Ghuznee and Kabul Medal 1841-42. Reverse Kandahar unnamed,
as issued with original steel clip and steel straight bar suspension NEF . . **£210**
South Africa medal 1877-79 2379 G. Broadbent 2-21st Foot Royal Scots
Fusiliers. Confirmed on roll. **£290**
Crimea 1854-56 Arch'd McFarlane, Scots Fusiliers **£150**

Gorget to the Old Comrade's Association 1920's **£195**
Iron Cross, War Merit Cross, Austrian Service Medal 1914-18 and Austro
Hungarian 1914-18 . . . . **£85**

MEDALS

Queen Elizabeth George Medal awarded to Rhodesian Police Inspector Maxwell for the rescue of three children from a crocodile attack. He was himself savaged by the crocodile as it tried to drag him into the water. He escaped by gouging out its eyes!........................ **£2,250**
DFC/DFM Aircrew Europe group to Sgt McMullan who flew Halifax bombers on numerous operations over enemy territory **£1,750**

Two groups of Saxon orders for sale as individual items.
Left: Order of Albert. Given by the King............................ **£550**
Knight's neck cross... **£550**
Knight's breast cross, with crown **£180**
Knight's breast cross, without crown **£110**
At the top in a Prussian Hohenzolleren loyalty order breast star **£650**
Right: Ernestine House Order. Top: Hohenzolleren House Order, breast star **£450**
Middle: 5th class breast cross, for lower ranks **£70**
5th class breast cross, for lower ranks. Boxed (pre 1914) **£80**
Top with ribbon. Commander's Cross **£800**
Below: Knight's breast cross...................................... **£350**

Top: WW1 DSM. 1914 Star WW1 pair. middle, French Merit Agricole.
Original cap badge. All to a colonel in the Royal Engineers. **£740**
Below: WW1 DCM, MM plus a 14/15 trio to a corporal in the 8th Seaforth Highlanders **£750**

A set of silver plated Iron Crosses awarded by Hitler to his generals after the Polish campaign.. **£850**
Imperial Iron Cross 2nd class with miniature...................... **£145**
German Cross in gold. In original case **£1,050**
Eagle Order 3rd class in its original case. Maker – Godet of Berlin **£850**

ORDNANCE

Back left to right: Modern Russian artillery shall case
1986 . . . . **£50**
British 105mm flat head tank proof round **£50**
American 76mm
OTO Malara round for a navy ship **£70**
British 20 pdr. tank A.P.D.S. drill round 1950's . . **£100**
British 105mm Howitzer drill round.
In current use 1970 . . . . **£55**
Shell case, Russian artillery, about 140mm **£40**
British 120mm tank A.P.D.S. practice projectile for
Chieftain tank. Current issue **£70**
Bottom left to right: British 18pdr shrapnel shell
1918 dated **£40**
British 76mm A.R.M.D. for Scorpion tank.
Inert instructional round **£75**
British WW2 1942 tank/anti tank 2pdr drill round,
made of wood and brass **£40**
British 40mm BOFORS breakup round.
Modern 1974 . . . . **£24**
British civilian WW2 gas mask in brass coloured
tin box. **£10**
Oe 35mm anti aircraft drill round **£30**
Next: as a before, ... **£30**
Oe 35mm anti aircraft drill round 1977. . . . . **£40**
American WW2 1942 37mm M16 A.P.C. round. . **NPA**
Oe 30mm K.C.B. drill round. 1987. . . . . **£15**

Left:
WWI hand grenades.
German **£35**
French **£35**
British Mills **£45**
German Egg. . . **£35**

Right:
American WW2
75mm Sherman tank
rounds, armour
piercing. Each . . **£40**

Left:
WW1 German 'Oyster Grenade'.
Designed to be thrown like a discus
to enable it to reach further **£45**

MISCELLANEOUS

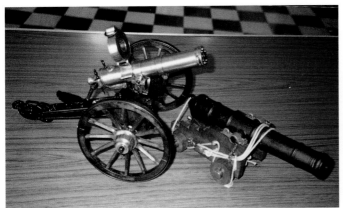

Model replica cannon. Gattling Gun **£50**
British Naval cannon. **£27**

A collection of German and Foreign Legion Steins. WW1 and WW2 in
porcelain and glass. From. . . . . **£35 – £85**

1917 dated military sextant by Stanley and Turnstile of London.
In its original leather case. **£95**

WWII British Astro compass. Dated 1945 Admiralty, in original wood box. . . **£40**

(left) WW2 German navigational instrument, from an E-boat. **£125**
(right) WW2 German M.G. 42 optical sight **£350**

UNIFORMS

1881 pattern officer's scarlet patrol jacket to the
Border Regiment (Volunteer Battalion).........**£150**
Early Sam Brown double brace rig.................**£50**
Other ranks artillery foreign service helmet ..**£125**

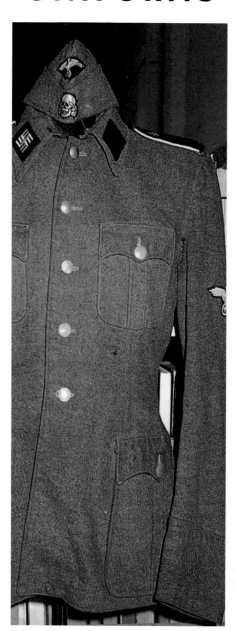

Complete WW2 German medical officer's
uniform. Includes tunic, breeches, cap, boots and
belt.................................**£750**

Above:
SS Camp guard's jacket,
including overseas cap.............................**$2,300**

Left:
Brigadier's uniform, named and dated in tunic,
H.S.K. Mainwaring October 1943.
Served in The Royal Hussars 1928-35, converted
to Royal Artillery 1939. Served in the Middle East
1939-45, Italy and Greece, General Staff 1st &
8th Army and the Brigadier General's Staff, Italy
and Greece, Southern Command. Tunic, cap,
trousers and greatcoat. VGC **£225**

Right:
Flying jacket – painted with Air Transport
Command – Kunming 1943.
Size 42, in good condition..............**£200**

UNIFORMS

RAF Warrant officer's tunic and cap. Pilot's wings, defence, war, general service and RAF long service bar. Possibly 1944 . . . . **£45**

WW2 Officer's 'pinks and greens', 8th Air Force. Captain's rank. Silver pin back Gemsco wing, D.F.C. and A.M. model ribbon bar **£215**
WW2 U.S. beaver fur crusher cap. New York maker **£125**
U.S. Airborne helmet, rigger made straps, named and numbered **£225**

WW2 U.S. W.A.C.
Uniform **£175**
A pair of shoes
for above **£55**

S.A. Brown Shirt inc. arm band. Early 1930s **£150**
Nuremburg rally badge **£6**

HEAD-DRESS

21st Lancers warrant officer's Czapska **£875**

WW2 U.S. Officer's visor cap. Felt construction, very good condition . . . **£65**

Hitler Youth Banner **£325**
S.A. Pennant **£195**
Police Shako **£295**

Trooper's helmet of the Kaiser's bodyguard, circa 1914 . . . . **£3,000**

HEAD-DRESS

S.S. officer's crusher cap. **£750**
S.S. officer's parade hat, named **£1,000**
Infantry NCO's Hat, named **£200**
S.S. sleeve eagles . . . . **£20** to **£50**
Totenkoff collar tab . . . . **£90** pair
S.S. sleeve arm band. **£55**
Estonian S.S. officer's parade belt **£500**

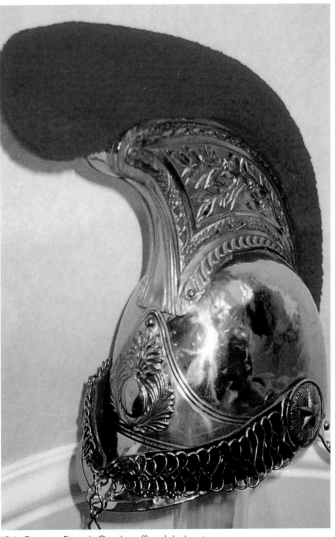

19th Century French Cavalry officer's helmet,
with original liner and comb **£855**

1950's Life Guards officer's helmet **£1,800**
Copy of French Napoleonic officer's Shako of 100th Regiment **£225**
Grenadier Guards bearskin – late 1940's **£200**

Turkish Janissay's Helmet. Sultan's bodyguard disbanded in 1826. . . . . . **£580**
Wahabite Arab dagger and belt. Solid silver with semi precious stones. . . . **£250**

EDGED WEAPONS

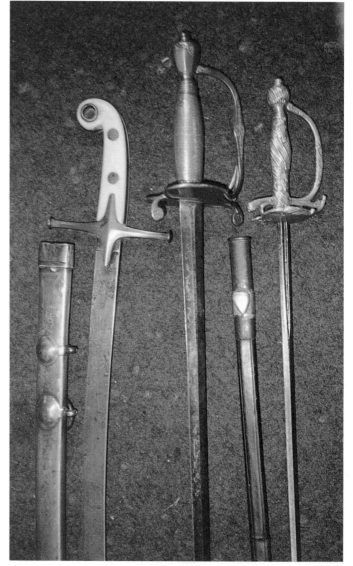

Lancaster bayonet. **£95**
Georgian band sword **£165**
Lancaster bayonet. **£165**
Regimental presentation Kukri, Edwardian **£125**
Standard German bayonet. **£65**
Hitler Youth knife **£65**
S.S. bayonet **£55**
Victorian Bowie knife. Ivory hilted. **£225**
Small Georgian dagger **£65**
2 bayonet frogs, each **£10**

Duke of Cumberland's Yeomanry Cavalry Mameluke, circa 1815. . . . . . **£500**
English heavy cavalry officer's dress sword 1796 . . . . **£350**
French or Spanish 'boy's' rapier circa 1760. . . . . **£300**

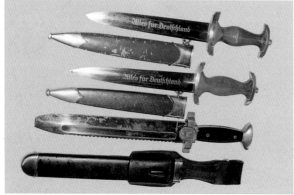

Two German S.A. daggers with scabbards, each **£150**
WW2 Red Cross man's sidearm and scabbard and frog **£150**

Bayonets:
S14 Bayard WW1 German. **£85**
German 'sawback' bayonet WW1. . . . . **£85**
S84/98 German 'sawback' bayonet WW1 . . . . **£95**
Demag German Esatz WW1 knife bayonet **£80**

EDGED WEAPONS

British 1879 pattern Martini Henry artillery carbine sword bayonet **£225**
WW2 Nazi mounted artillery officer's sword. **£250**
Sheffield Bowie knife. **£120**

Mid seventeenth century Cromwellian mortuary back sword, with single
edge. So called, it is thought because after the execution of Charles 1, some
were chiselled with the King's head on the guard **£550**
17th century Spanish cup hilt rapier with blade of shallow diamond section,
made by Francisco Ruis of Toledo. Cup chiselled with naive horsemen. . **£1,250**

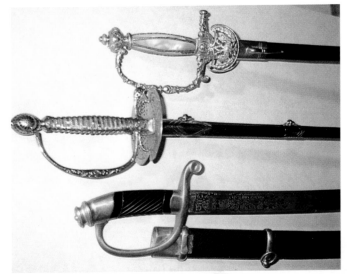

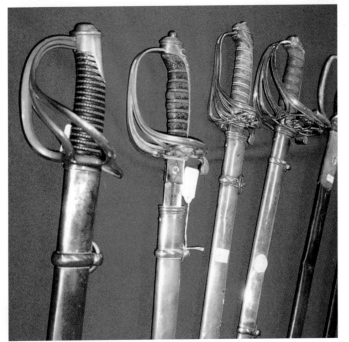

Imperial Russian officer's presentation sword with its original gilding, 1880
Georgian cut steel 1775, Imperial Russian diplomat corps sword 1860 – 1870
All above, each **£1,000**

Sabres and swords from 1822 onwards.
American and British priced from **£149**

FIREARMS

Broom Handled Mauser pistol with wooden stock. German dated 1896
(deactivated) **£200**

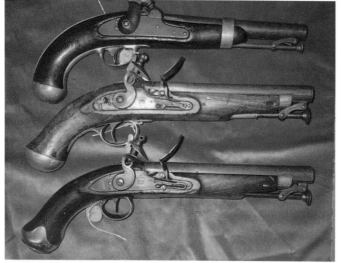

US marshall pistol 1864 . . . . **£355**
William IV British military pistol **£850**
Newland pattern British military flintlock pistol **£850**

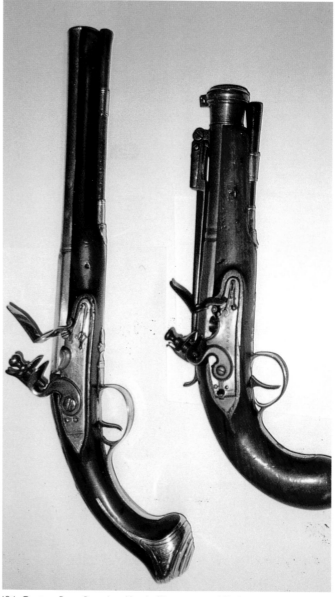

18th Century Brass Barrel and Lock, Silver mounted flintlock by Burnford of
London Blunderbuss Barrelled Flintlock Pistol by Henry Nock with top spring
Bayonet. Circa 1800 . . . . **£1,650**

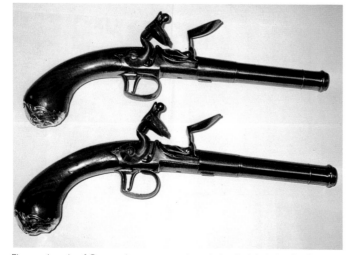

Fine early pair of Queen Anne cannon barrel pistols. Made by Griffin of
London. With walnut stocks and silver grotesque butt caps, circa 1750 . . **£2,450**

.31 Pocket pistol by Bacon Manufacturing Company.
Only 900 of these were made **£385**

FIREARMS

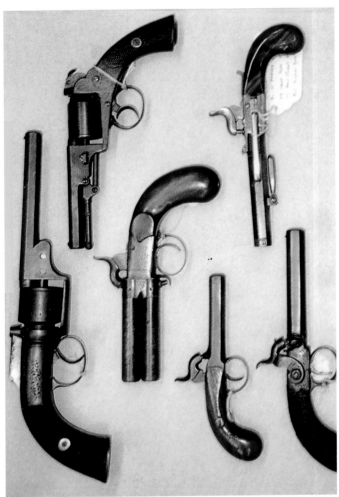

A pair of Queen Anne cannon barrelled pocket pistols. Silver inlay hallmarked
1783. Pair £1,395
Remington Rider .32 rim firer 1858. . . . . £340

English transitional revolver circa 1840 . . . . **£345**
English Bentley & Playfair revolver circa 1855 . . . . **£225**
Irish O'Harrold of Dundalk. Double barrelled pistol **£265**
Belgian with English proofs travelling pistol **£130**
English Parker of London "Turn off" pistol. **£375**
English Birmingham travelling pistol **£165**

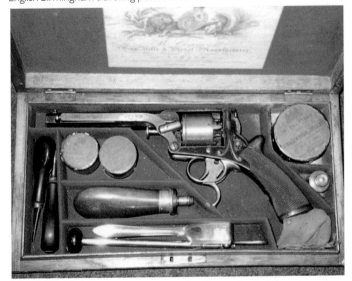

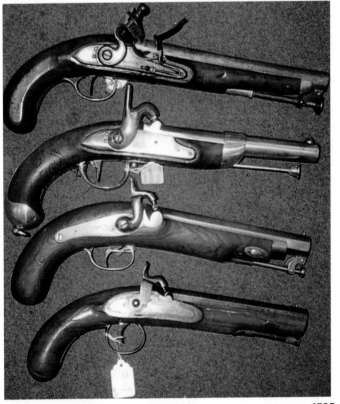

Cased double tripper 3rd model Tranter by Cogswell of London, circa 1862.
Includes all original accessories. Bullet mould is numbered to gun **£1,750**

British military pistol by H. Nock. Early 1800s **£595**
French percussion pistol 1840s **£475**
Imported Indian-type good quality percussion pistol 1850's **£200**
Percussion pistol, by Waterhouse and Horton 1835 . . . . **£550**

BADGES

Australian Shoulder Titles:
With borders. 1948-76.
Without Borders 1967-90, from (in Aust $) **$5**
WW2 colour patches, from . . . . **$8 - $15**
RMC Duntroon Colour Party Crossed Flags **$55**
RACT Air Dispatch Wings, bullion. **$45**
Cloth **$25**

Various badges and belt clips.
i.e. Piper's badge – Irish Guards **£90**
6th West York Militia Officer's waist belt clasp **£75**

Various badges: 1st Vol. Bat. Durham Light Infantry **£70**
Liverpool Rifle Brigade **£85**
Scots Guards Pipers **£35**

Nazi cloth badges . . . . **£5 – £25**

BADGES

Shoulder emblems of the former Yugoslavia. i.e. Bosnian, Croatian, Bosnian Muslim, Serbian and Croatian. From .... **£10** upwards

Nazi badges and memorabilia. i.e. Tie pins from .... **£15 – 330**
Breast eagles from .... **£11 – £85**
Cap eagles from **£20**

Early S.A. cloth collar patches 1925 to 1940. Priced from **£50**

Brigade of Guards Colour Sergeant's arm badges **£18**
RSM badge, Brigade of Guards **£50**

Various cloth shoulder titles. WWII to present from............. **£1 – £3**

Just some of the many thousands of shells which appear each year in France and Belgium.

Crapouillot mortar found in Ablaincourt Pressoir near Chaulne by a farmer with his plough twelve years ago. It fires 25kg bombs.

A 1916 Saint Etienne French machine gun found at Sailly Saillisel France.

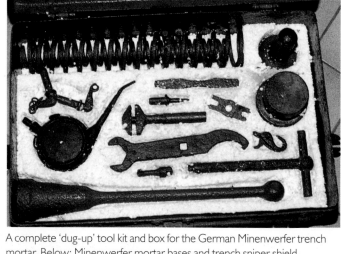

A complete 'dug-up' tool kit and box for the German Minenwerfer trench mortar. Below: Minenwerfer mortar bases and trench sniper shield.

A collection of relic pistols found near Ytres.

BADGES

Badge collectors can be sure of finding plenty of choice at almost any event, for insignia collecting remains one of the most popular aspects of militaria.

In the late 17th century, standardisation of uniforms in order to reinforce 'corporate' identity was extended to fastenings such as buckles, buttons and headdress plates. At first many of these items bore the royal cypher, or in some cases, the coat of arms of the aristocrat who had raised the regiment and equipped it at his own expense. Later they were designed to contain regimental information; and because of the continuing process of change and development among the armed forces over the years, so new patterns of insignia evolved. Designs of badges and buttons, helmet and belt plates, and cloth patches, have been refined to a high degree, offering a cornucopia of collecting interest, so that the enthusiast can now choose from thousands of items costing almost nothing to single pieces worth many hundreds of pounds or dollars.

The cap badge, which has been in existence for around a hundred years, is one of the most popular insignia, particularly in the UK and Commonwealth (or former Commonwealth) countries. Made of white metal, brass, plastic or 'Staybrite' (anodized aluminium) at various periods of its history, it was often one of the few items that servicemen kept and thus offers the potential for collecting by regiment, arm of service, county, period of history and so on. Collections of cap badges, which often began as a pocket-money hobby for schoolboys between the wars and in the 1950s, are now fetching seriously adult prices. However, there are a great many 're-strikes' on the market so that collectors wanting only a genuine contemporary item should do their homework first.

Other examples of metal insignia – collar dogs, helmet plates, shoulder titles and buttons, are all readily available, and have the added advantages of not requiring a great deal of room and being easy to display.

There are also many unusual badges worth seeking out such as the metal and enamel badges issued for war work during the First World War, the demand for which was a result of the 'white feather' campaign by some militant women towards men not in uniform. Sweetheart brooches in regimental designs, popular during the two World Wars, are also to be found at most collectors' events.

Military and political badges of the German Third Reich offer enormous scope to the collector worldwide – as well as much heart-searching; because they are increasingly reproduced, the buyer should be on his guard, arm himself with as much information as possible, talk to experienced collectors and buy from a reputable source. The badges produced for soldiers who saw action, for example infantry or tank assault badges, are particularly popular, especially when accompanied by any paperwork such as a soldbuch, as are the various degrees of wound badge.

Cloth patches became a notable feature of American insignia following the First World War. Colourful and elaborate patches can be found for all branches of US armed forces, including police – and even for a participant's part in the space programme. Ironically, troops serving in Vietnam found the eye-catching colours of the standard cloth patches a dangerous liability in jungle warfare and this led to the production of locally made subdued cloth insignia, examples of which now command high prices from collectors. Second World War cloth insignia, especially to Special Forces units, is also much in demand.

The following pictures illustrate the enormous range and prices of insignia available on the market today.

Officer's pouch belt badge, circa 1870, of the 2nd Sikh Infantry (Punjab Frontier Force), VGC . . . **£410**

Selection of WWII divisional signs from **£4**

Medal ribbon bars, stick pins and day badges to the German political and armed forces from . . **£5**

WWII patches . . . . **US $5 – 20**

Imperial German Navy observer's badge **£70**
A WWII Free Czech Airforce pilot's badge, in silver, triple clip rear attachment **£195**
Imperial German pilot's badge, solid back with rayed panel, pin stamped '800' **£190**
Scarce Royal Yugoslav silver pilot's badge, in 925 silver, back marked Beograd, screw wheel attachment **£80**
Imperial Austrian army field pilot's badge, in gilt and enamels, by Zingler Wien, cypher of Franz Josef . **£85**
Nazi tank battle badge with panel for 50 engagements, maker JFS, silvered wreath . . **£420**
Nazi blockade runner's badge, trace of maker "Fec Otto Plackek Berlin", ... **£40**
Nazi E Boat badge (1st type) **£125**

A selection of U.S. law enforcement badges (current issue) from **£20**

Arm badges as worn by 2GR Gurkhas 1960-94 from Vietnam to the present day . . . . **NPA**

FURTHER READING:
Collecting Military Antiques
by Frederick Wilkinson
Published by Bracken Books 1984

Military Badge Collecting
by John Gaylor – Pub. Leo Cooper 1996

Australian hat badges.
Post 1960 from . . . . **AUS $8 – $25**

Other ranks helmet plate to the Lifeguards 1902 to 1952 . . . . **£112**
Lifeguard's waist belt clasp 1953 . . . . **£100**
Edward VII waist belt clasp **£65**

A selection of officer's Boss badges.
WWI to present day, ranging from . . . . . **£15 – 35**

Nazi tank battle badge, with panel for 25 engagements, hollow back, maker "G.B"..£320

Presidential Inauguration badge, issued by The Maryland State Police (George Bush)...£185

Various badges: Royal Irish Rifles each	£12
Scottish Rifles officer's Shako badge	£15
Duke of Cambridge's Light Cavalry pouch badge (German silver)	£25
Royal Artillery helmet plate	£12
Worcestershire Regiment pouch badge	£8
Hertfordshire helmet plate	£15
The Highlanders (silver plated)	£8

Various Third Reich and Imperial German awards and qualification badges. From..£30 – £800

British battledress shoulder titles. 1939/40 until 1952. Each.............£3

German Bronze S.A. (Sturm Abteilung) Sports Badge, circa 1934 .....£35
D.R.L. Sports Badge, circa 1937 ....£35

A Victorian officer's gilt and silver plated HP of The Royal Marines Light Infantry, blue enamel backing to motto, good condition **£260**

Royal Regiment of Fusiliers badge **£35**

Royal Marines slip-on rank insignia. Colour Sergeant **£5**
Corporal **£4**
Lance Corporal **£3.50**

1st class Baltic Cross in case, issued by Germany prior to WWII for service in the Baltic. **£70**

Assorted German badges and insignia. WWII period . . . . **£8 – £30**

Various badges including, middle:
Rifle Brigade Cross Belt plate 1877 in hallmarked silver **£185**
Mid left: Officer's helmet plate. West Indian Regiment. Victorian **£250**
Bottom left: Plaid Brooch. 3rd Vol. Battalion Northumberland Fusiliers, circa 1904, in hallmarked silver . . . **£1,200**

Reproduction L.A.P.D. police badge **£85**
Hawaii police force . **£50**

Australian army hat badges. (Aust $) Left to right:

7th Infantry Regiment 1903-12. Brass	**$300**
70th Infantry Regiment 1912-18. Brass	**$650**
Staff Corps. 1921 pattern. Enamelled	**$150**
Victorian Rangers. 1903-12. 2nd Pattern. Brass	**$180**
Victorian Defence Force Infantry. Pre-1901. Brass	**$140**
Staff Corps. 1921 pattern. Cap Size. Enamelled	**$110**
23rd Light Horse. 1930-42. Brass	**$65**
1st Armoured Car Regiment. 1930-42. Brass	**$150**
4th Infantry Bn. 1930-42. Brass	**$110**
7/21st Light Horse. 1953-60. W/M.	**$70**
32nd Infantry Battalion. 1930-42. Brass	**$35**
Victoria Volunteer Cadet Corps. Pre-1901. Brass	**$45**
Medical Corps. 1930-42. Brass	**$25**
Commonwealth Cadet Corps. Victoria. 1906. Brass	**$35**
59th Infantry Bn. 1930-42. Enamelled	**$35**
58th Infantry Bn. (E.C.B.) 1930-42. Enamelled	**$35**

A selection of French Foreign Legion badges:
Including, Amphibious training centre badge (on Madagascar) 1971 . . . . . **£20**
Companie de Protection 2nd REI/1st rec Desert Storm. Only approx 250 issued (for guarding prisoners of war taken from Iraq) **£150**

Set of three wound badges, Gold, Silver and Bronze for the 20th July 1944 all presented by Hitler reverse marked 800 and stamped 1, part of only 100 made, condition excellent . . . . **US $20,000**

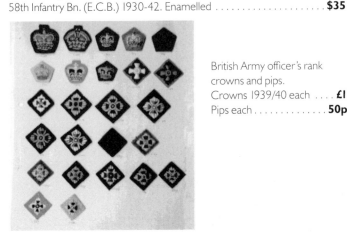

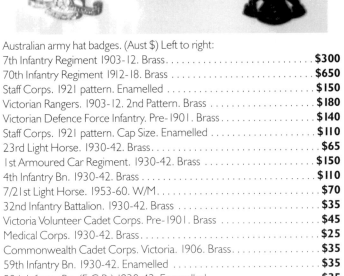

British Army officer's rank crowns and pips.
Crowns 1939/40 each **£1**
Pips each **50p**

WWII U.S. Army Airforce badges.
Cloth with silk embroidery each **£2.50**
Cloth with wire embroidery **£5**

A collection of Russian enamel badges. Prices from **50p – £1.50**

A selection of cross belt and piper's badges:
Including: 4th Battalion South Lancs Regiment, post 1952 . . . . **£175**
Victorian Piper's, Connaught Rangers **£35**

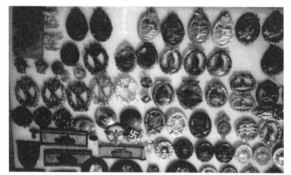

Various items of German insignia and awards:
Including tank destruction strip (lower centre) Prices from **£30**

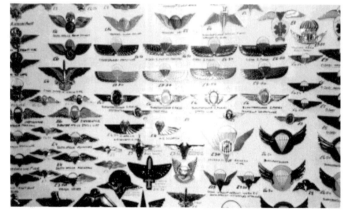

Southern Africa parachute wings from **£3**

Right: Silver Wounds Badge
(Verwound Abzeichen). **£16**

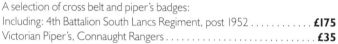

Cloth formation badges. All WWII. Top row, left to right.
7th Indian Division **£25**
404th Indian District **£45**
303rd Indian District **£45**
Middle row: British 6th Infantry Division **£30**
88 A.G.R.A. British post war **£30**
21st Indian Corps **£30**
Bottom row: British 8th Armoured Division **£25**
101st Armoured Brigade **£45**
1st Armoured Division **£25**

FURTHER READING:
Head-dress Badges of the British Army
Vol 1 & 2. *A. L. Kipling and H. L. King*
Published by Hugh King

German 1st. Class War Merit Cross, with swords, 1939 onwards **£60**
Bronze Army driver's badge. 1939 onwards **£28**

Australian Police and Fire Brigade badges. (Aust $)
Top: Northern Territory Police Cadet **$400**
Right: Australian Capital Territory Fire Brigade **$45**
Left: Queensland Fire Service **$45**
Bottom: West Australia Police **$150**

Top row: Edinburgh City Artillery grenade badge 1880 . . . . **£130**
Officer's shoulder belt plate to the 10th Gurkhas in silver, circa 1908 . . . . **£75**
Quilted Shako to the 6th foot Warwicks, circa 1870 . . . . **£80**
Bottom: Officer's Glengarry badge to the York and Lancs, circa 1896. . . **£140**
Glengarry badge to the Leicester Militia. **£110**

Top to bottom: S.S. cuff title (flag company) . . . . **NPA**
Political Leader's armband with white piping. **£125**
Fragment of Messerschmidt, Battle of Britain souvenir **£15**
Various field postcards, each. **£4**

Top left to right: Victorian officer's helmet plate of the Bedfordshire Reg. . . . **£170**
Pouch belt badge of the Monmouthshire Regiment, (post 1920) **£60**
A trooper's helmet plate, 5th Dragoon Guards, circa 1900. . . . . **£75**
Bottom left to right. Victorian helmet plate, New Zealand Volunteers . . . **£35**
Pair of officer's collar badges of the Kings Liverpool Regiment. Victorian . **£50**
A post 1908 officer's helmet plate of the Territorial Artillery **£50**

British Royal Marine full
dress stripes
Single: **£1.50**
Double: **£2.50**
Treble: **£3.50**

Badges, top left: WWII
German Infantry Assault
Badge, Bronze Class . . **£70**
Right: General Assault
Badge **£45**
Below left: Infantry Assault
Badge. Silver **£55**
Right: Wound Badge,
in black. **£15**

FURTHER READING:
Rifle Volunteer Buttons 1859-1908.
by *Howard Ripley & Denis Darmanin*
Published by Military Historical Society

Collecting Military Shoulder Titles
by *Ray Westlake*
Published by Pen and Sword

Australian miscellaneous badges and patches. WWII onward . . . **AUS $5 – $45**

Australian cloth patches. Pre WWI to modern, from . . . . **AUS $8 – $25**

Australian Army and Police Badges: (Aust $)
41st Infantry Battalion, 1930-42. Brass. $450
23rd Infantry Battalion, 1930-42. Brass $250
45th Infantry Battalion, 1930-42. Brass $150
18th Light Horse, 1930-42. Brass $130
46th Brighton Rifles, 1912-18. Brass $250
12th Launceston Infantry, 1903-12. Cap size. Brass $100
16th Light Horse. 1930-42, W/M $200
30th NSW Scottish. 1930-42, W/M $150
Tank Corps. 1930-42, brass $450
Northern Territory Police, nickel & enamel $400
13th Light Horse. 1930-42, W/M $300
22nd Infantry Bn. 1930-42, brass $220
52nd Infantry Bn. 1930-42,. (2nd pattern), green enamel $300
11th Light Horse. 1930-42. W/M $140
Victorian Railway Infantry. 1903-12. W/M $150
WWI Volunteered for Active Service – Medically Unfit, lapel badge,
silvered brass $35

Dr. Fritz Todt award from WWII . . . . S. African Rand **R2,750**

Helmet plate (left) for
the Maritzburg Rifles
(pre-1887) Natal Royal
Rifles 1889
(the pair) **R2,750**
(South African Rand)

EDGED WEAPONS

The search for a perfect sword, one which combines the qualities of cut and thrust, with strength, balance and aesthetics, has engaged sword makers for centuries and resulted in the large variety of designs that can be found at military collectors' events the world over.

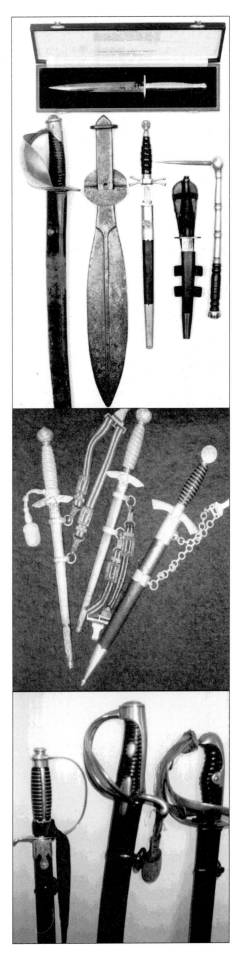

Among the earlier regulation swords for infantry and cavalry are the 1796 patterns which are available and desirable as they armed the soldiers of the Napoleonic Wars. There is therefore more likelihood that such weapons saw action on the battlefield rather than being carried as ceremonial items. Prices range from under £100 to about £300 for a trooper's sword in good condition. Officers' blued and gilt swords from this period are more expensive, especially if they come with some provenance – provided the owner was not a desk-bound warrior! A good 1796 'heavy' cavalry officer's sword sells for as much £1200.

Other sought-after swords include those that can be associated with historic events. The film Braveheart, for example, and the 250th anniversary of the battle of Culloden have brought increased interest in Scottish basket-hilted broadswords.

Japanese swords form a distinct collecting niche which can be bewildering for beginners. It is a prolific area, however, as it has been estimated that between 1350 and 1850 there were 30,000 sword makers in Japan. Second World War swords are also readily available and largely manufactured in the same traditional way as early blades.

Bayonets are extremely popular as well as being, by and large, a safe collecting field with few pitfalls for the unwary. First introduced as hunting weapons and later adapted for military use, the earliest ones simply plugged into the muzzle of a firearm. This crude but effective solution to the problem of what to do when the musket had been fired changed battlefield tactics and led to the demise of the pikeman. Although many thousands were produced from the mid-17th century onwards, plug bayonets are rarely seen at collectors' events today. Their later incarnation, the socket bayonet, is prolific, however, and offers a large variety of styles, from the 30-inch-long Jacob's sword bayonet to the 7-inch spike bayonet for the Lee Enfield No. 4 rifle.

Although British, German and French bayonets are popular, up and coming is the interest in Commonwealth variants of standard British patterns and also in Indian-pattern bayonets. In the UK, demand for bayonets from other countries is growing as collectors visit large fairs to buy and take back their heritage. Prices vary typically from £10 to £100, although many of the scarcer 19th- century British and German bayonets can cost between £100 and £500.

Other edged weapons include many varieties of combat knives from the Thugee weapons of India, through machetes and kris to the Bowie knife of American fame, although the pending legislation on the sale and possession of combat knives in the UK is having a depressive effect on the market for these items.

FURTHER READING:
Swords of the British Army *by Brian Robson* Published by The National Army Museum

British and Commonwealth Bayonets *by Ian D. Skennerton and Robert Richardson* Published by Selous Books Ltd

Japanese Military and Civil Swords and Dirks *by Richard Fuller and Ron Gregory* Published by Airlife Publishing Ltd.

Kris with wooden sheath on wooden mount with commemorative plaque. Given to Major R.N. Campbell A. & S.H. by the sergeant's mess 1967 . . **NPA**

Swept hilt rapier and companion left hand dagger by Antonio Picinic. (inscribed on blade). Circa 1600, pair **£7,000**

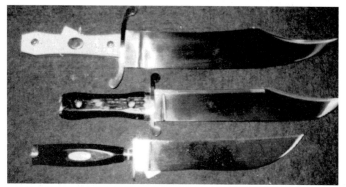

Top: 1850's pattern hand forged Bowie knife as used in Texas **£135**
Middle: "Iron Mistress" Exact replica of the knife made for the film in 1951 . . **£125**
Bottom: Exact copy of the 1835 Resin Bowie knife, Alamo period, as on display in the Alamo **£145**

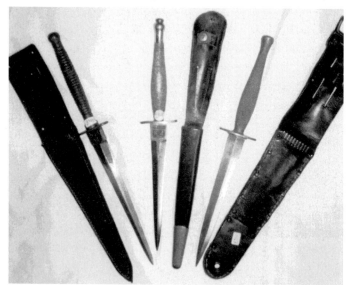

Left to right: U.S. Marine Corps stiletto by Camillus. 1944 . . . . **£750**
F.S. 1st pattern British commando knife by Wilkinson Sword. 1941 . . . . **£325**
Australian commando knife as used by Z Force in the Far East, circa 1942 . . . . **£550**

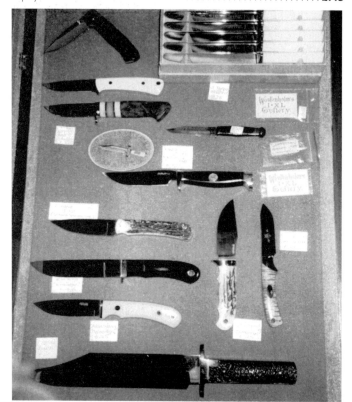

A selection of modern hand made knives:
Randall (USA) RKS Club Knife **£325**
Alan Wood 'Wanderer' **£145**
Alan Wood 'Woodlore' **£125**
R. Johnson Semi Skinner. **£170**
B. Levingood Woodcraft **£125**
P. Henry Bowie **£110**

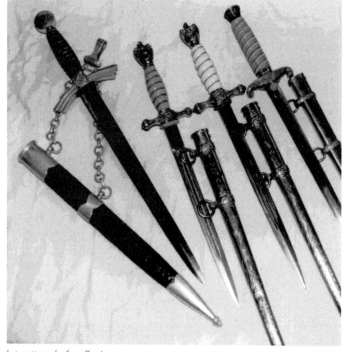

1st pattern Luftwaffe dagger **£200**
2 x Kriegsmarine daggers, each **£175**
German army dagger **£150**

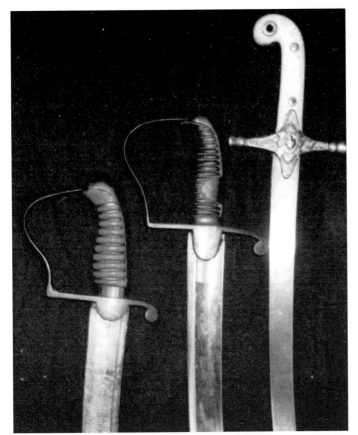

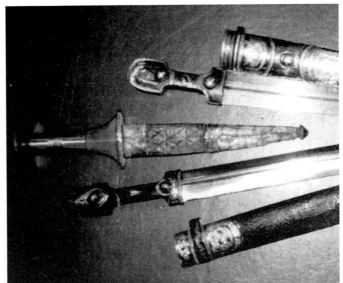

Scottish Mameluke. Ivory hilted **£225**
1796 Light cavalry sabre. **£250**
1796 Light cavalry sabre including scabbard **£275**

Victorian naval officer's sword, supplied with complete history **£450**
British George III 1803 pattern light company officer's sword **£160**
British George III side arm **£125**

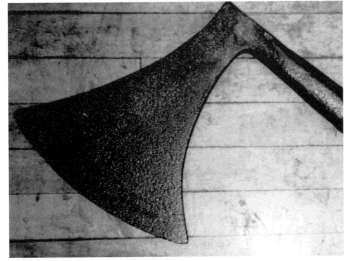

Headsman's Axe, mid 16th century, probably German **£1,400**

Scottish Dirks: 19th century . . . . **£600 – £1,600**
Skean-Dhu. . . . . **£50 – 3160**

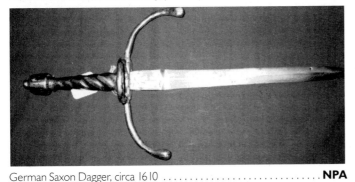

German Saxon Dagger, circa 1610 . . . . **NPA**

Swords: French circa 1600 . . . . **£650**
Indian early 19th century . . . . **£35 – £1,350**
Shield: Indian later 18th century **£325**

A collection of Nazi Hitler Youth daggers priced from . . . . **£65 – £120**

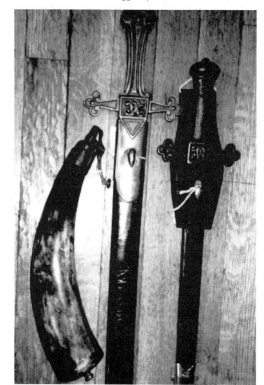

English brass mounted gunner's powder horn 19th century **£85**
British Victorian band sword **£95**

Malay Kris holder and Kris **£175**

Original Bowie knife in display case . . . . **NPA**

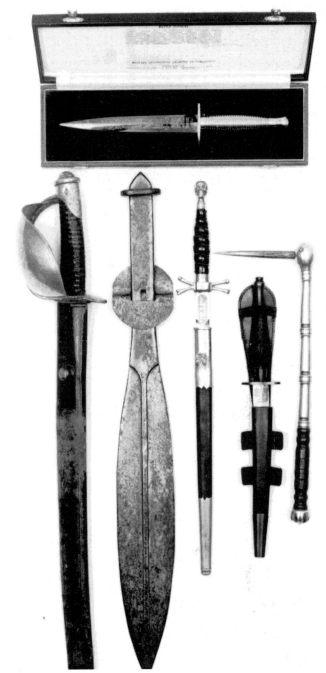

19th century silver mounted bade-bade, 8¼" slender SE blade 5¾", foliate engraved silver hilt. In its wooden sheath, foliate engraved silver mounts, foliate carved rhino horn top. **£95**
Early Java kris, 7¾" slightly swollen blade 13½" with raised central rib, some pamor grain. Silver cup, finely incised Palembang ivory garuda hilt of foliate designs, in its well grained wooden sheath, silver chape. **£250**
19th century Malay kris, broad wavy pamor blade 18¼" wooden hilt nicely carved with a stylised elephant's head covered with intricate foliage, silver cup. It its wooden sheath. **£160**
An attractive Bali kris, wavy black and silver pamor blade 18¼" black hardwood hilt carved as a dancing demonic figure, small paste set ferrule, in its wooden sheath. **£210**
19th century Malay peninsula kris, 18¾" broad swollen pamor blade 12¾" of good pattern, foliate chiselled Bugis cup, wooden garuda hilt. In its kemuning wooden sheath of good grain with ivory tip. **£160**
Early Java kris, swollen blade 13" with well pronounced "herringbone" pamor. Silver cup, ivory hilt carved with flowers and foliage overall in high relief, in its nicely grained wooden sheath with ivory tip **£330**
19th century Malayan dagger bade-bade, 10" curved SE blade 6¾" one piece hippopotamus tusk scroll carved pommel, in its nicely grained wooden sheath with hippo tusk finial **£85**

U.S. Civil War boarding cutlass	**£450**
Welsh WWI sword.	**£210**
Society dagger.	**£80**
Wilkinson F.S. knife	**£150**
Battle axe/pick	**£160**

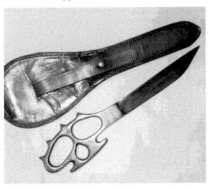

Rare British WWII Middle East commando knife, also known as the Death's Head knife, because the brass knuckle guard resembles a skull. A change in the UK law has prevented the manufacture, sale and export of this type of weapon. This knife was only issued to two units of about 1,200 men. Approx value **£220**

Nazi naval officer's dirk, by F.W. Holler, blade retaining some original polish, etched with fouled anchor, sailing ships and foliage, gilt brass mounts, wire bound white celluloid grip, original dress knot tied naval style, in its brass sheath with original black velvet lined hanging straps with gilt lion's mask buckles. (one swivel clip missing) **£330**

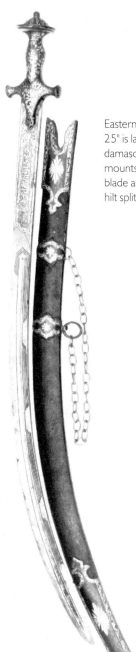

Eastern sword tulwar, blade 32¾", the front 25" is lap welded to a later section and gold damascened, en-suite with hilt and scabbard mounts. Inscriptions gold damascened to blade and hilt. (one hanging ring missing, hilt split at seam) £530

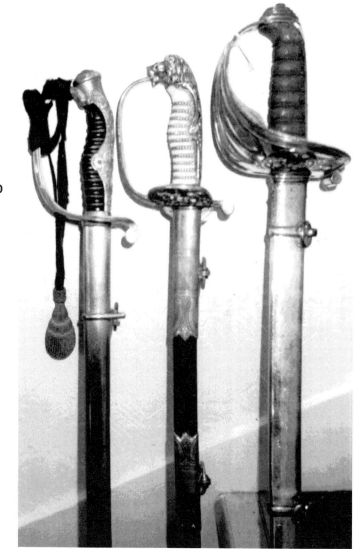

WW2 Japanese parade sword £165
Imperial German naval officer's sword £375
English 1837 rifle volunteer's sword £295

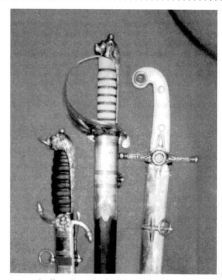

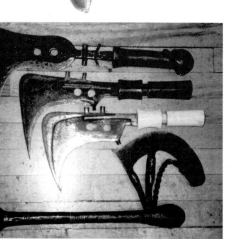

Mangito Axes: Top to bottom £175, £150, £300
Shono Axe £200

British pattern general officer's sword 1831 . . . . £159
British regulation naval officer's sword,
current issue £159
British pattern naval dirk £85

French AN XIII cuirassier's sword, double fullered blade 37", engraved on backstrap "Manufre Imple Du Klingenthal Mai 1812", brass hilt, brass wire bound leather covered grip, in its steel scabbard **£500**

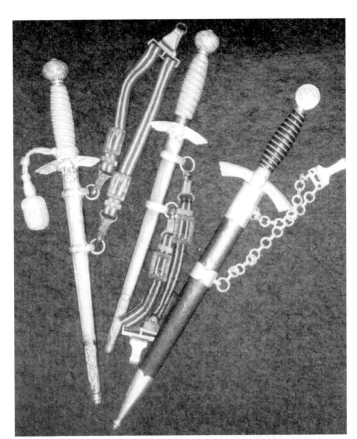

Orange handled 2nd pattern Luftwaffe dress daggers. WWII 3rd Reich period. Each **£275**
1st pattern Luftwaffe aluminium dress dagger. **£295**

Presentation Gurkha knives and badges on mounting shield **£15**

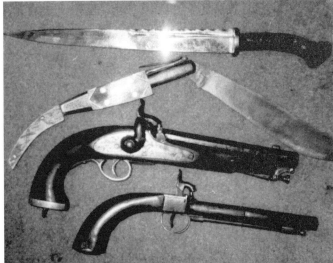

Scottish dirk 19th century **£45**
Folding knife, possibly Spanish,
turn of the century **£120**
English percussion pistol, circa 1880 . . . . **£120**
Belgian overcoat pistol, circa 1880. . . . . **£90**

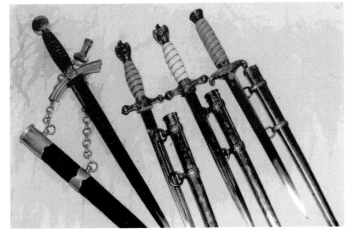

1st pattern Luftwaffe dagger **£200**
2 x Kriegsmarine daggers, each **£175**
German army dagger **£150**

Rare British Homeguard pikehead/machete, made in 1940 by Martindale . . . **£50**

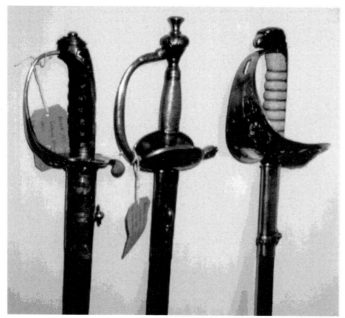

Swords: left to right;
British 1822 pattern infantry officer's sword. Blade by Thirkle. **£235**
Mid 19th century Prussian guards officer's sword by Geer Weyersberg of
Solingen **£295**
WWI R.A.F. pilot's dress sword **£395**

Saxon left handed dagger, circa 1600 . . . . **£700**
Turkish Jambia. Silver mounted with walrus ivory hilt **£800**
Scottish dirk with silver mountings, 1901 . . . . **£800**

WW2 Air Corps officer's jacket . . . . **US $100**
Civil War sabres. . . . . **US $300 – $500**

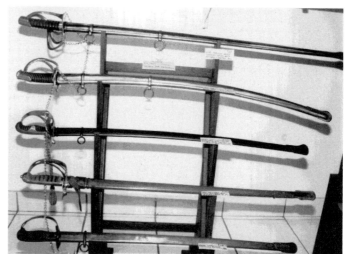

Swords: . . . . Prices in South African Rand
1801/02 pattern heavy cavalry (dated 1814) **R4,500**
1886 Japanese cavalry sabre **R2,850**

M1918 Camouflage helmet, complete with leather liner . . . . **2,500 FF**
German bayonets 98/05 pattern sawback . . . . **800 FF**

Imperial German double sided embroidered banner, dated 1900 . . . . . **£800**
Imperial Naval dress dirk. WWI **£750**
German superior quality hunting cutlass. Ivory hilted, damascus bladed,
with skinning knife. **£2,000**

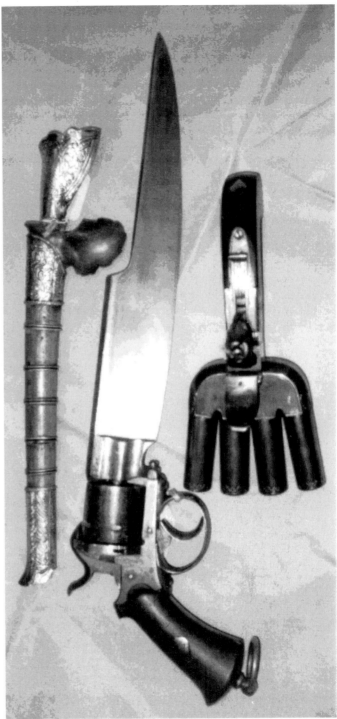

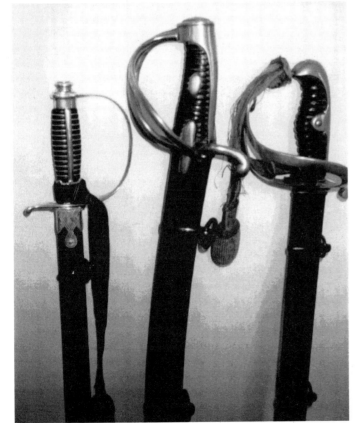

Malaysian kris. Silver and bone mounted, 19th century **£85**
Pin firing revolver with built-in knife, mid to late 1800s **£985**
Duck's foot flintlock pistol. Interesting historical details engraved on metal.
1800 by H. Nock of London. **£1,250**

German WW2 police sword. **£350**
Napoleonic sword 1812 . . . . **£500**
German imperial sword "RHEIN. TRAIN, BAT. No8" engraved on blade.
Pre-WWI **£350**

Rare model 38 Beretta folding bayonet (1938) . . . . S. African Rand **R1,560**

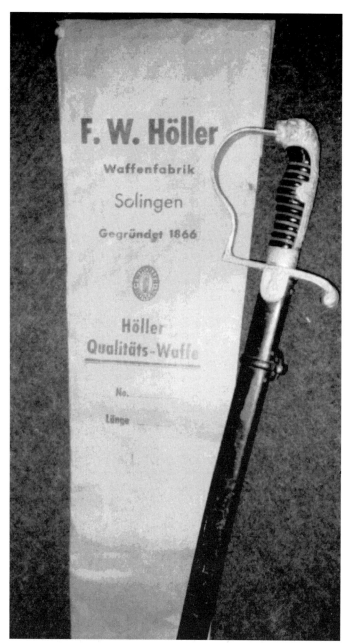

3rd Reich army officer's puma head sword. Unissued with original factory paper bag 1936. . . . . **£350**

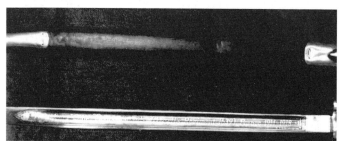

Presentation 1907 Lee Enfield bayonet. Issue marks 1945 but inscription for WWI and probably by Wilkinson. It reads "1st Battalion The Scots Guards" (Argyll's Regiment 1939) France 1914-1918 . . . . S. African Rand **R2,500**

FURTHER READING:
World Bayonets *by Anthony Carter*
Arms and Armour Press

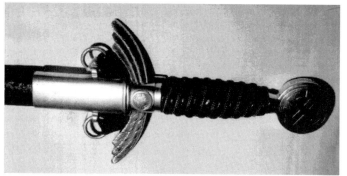

Luftwaffe officer's sword. VGC **£365**

Cutlery handled Bowie knife by H.R. Hounam of Sheffield, circa 1850 . . . **£450**

Assorted bayonets:
British cruciform bayonet No 4 Mark I made by Singer Sewing Machine Company 1939 . . . . **£50**
Imperial German 'sawback' butcher's bayonet **£75**
KS98 'sawback' butcher's bayonet **£75**
American Garand bayonet 1942 . . . . **£85**

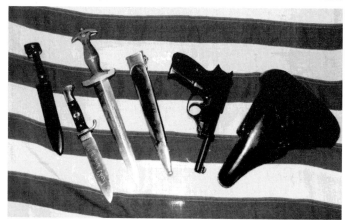

Hitler Youth dagger **£60**
S.A. dagger **£85**
P.38 pistol (deactivated) **£230**
Luger holster. **£65**

Various swords including: U.S. Civil War, rare light infantry sabre by Mansfield & Lamb of Forest Dale, Rhode Island 1864. . . . . **£250**

Ornamental Arabic knife in silver with overlaid scabbard and mounts. Circa 1850 . . . . **£55**

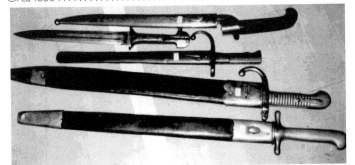

French hunting bayonet, circa 1850. . . . . **£525**
Serbian Mauser bayonet, circa 1940 . . . . **£650**
2nd pattern Japanese Murata 1888. . . . . **£450**
Belgium Terssen engineers sawback bayonet 1868. . . . . **£90**
Piedmontese (Italian state) sword bayonet 1837 . . . . **£345**

Tips for collectors

Bayonets are mass produced items so never rush to buy examples in poor condition – there will always be another one, usually at the same fair! Always buy examples in scabbards, as lack of a scabbard can halve the value.

WW2 Game of Air Sea Rescue, boxed with counters and instructions . . . **£55**
WWII British Commando dagger in leather sheath. Blade etched for member of the U.S. Army Airforce **£175**
Solid rubber instruction model of a Beaufort Bomber **£20**

Nazi party flag **£55**
R.A.D. man's dagger late 1930s **£375**
S.S. Parade fez. Bevo woven insignia, as used by Muslim troops attached to the Waffen S.S.. . . . . **NPA**
Car pennant for S.S.F.M.
(the organisation that collected money and funds for the S.S.). **£450**
S.S. officer's Adolf Hitler bullion hand embroidered cuff title (shortened) . . . **£295**
R.Z.M. type Waffen S.S. Polizei Division cuff. **£395**

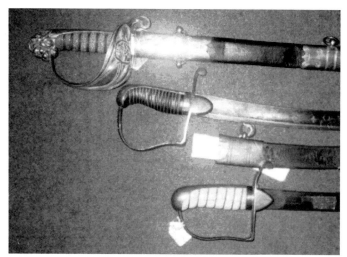

Top to bottom: British officer's sword 1827 pattern with markings for
George IV. **£290**
British Light Cavalry Sabre of pre 1796 pattern, probably around 1788 . **£315**
Officer's Light Cavalry Sabre, Indian Army, around 1830-40 . . . . **£125**

Knobkerries from the Zulu War, largest with carved handle **£55**
Two smaller ones, each **£45**

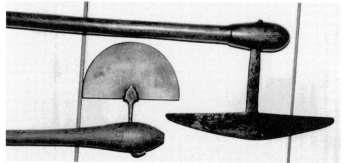

Zulu battle axes: . . . . Prices in South African Rand
Left: dated c. 1870 . . . . **R3,000**
Right: Turn of the century. The numbers 1937 refer to the date of a famous
murder trial of that date in which this was an exhibit **R2,000**

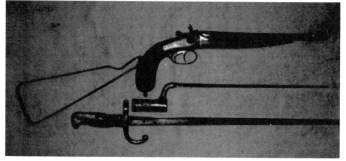

Bayonets from **£3.50**

Belgium 410 pistol with optional removable stock. It has a short barrel, so is
classed as a section one firearm **£120**
British Brown Bess bayonet, late 19th century **£25**
French sword bayonet inscribed on blade
"Mre D'Armes de Chât 4 Août 1876 . . . . **£20**

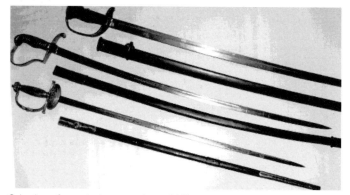

Selection of swords, Japanese, Imperial German,
Victorian Royal Household . . . . **NPA**

Tips for collectors

Copies are known to exist for many plug bayonets, the Farquar-Hill,
the Sappers and Miners, the Vivian Carbine, the Australian machete
bayonet, and the Elcho bayonet. Others, for example Brown Bess
socket and Baker Rifle bayonets, have been reproduced for the re-
enacting market.

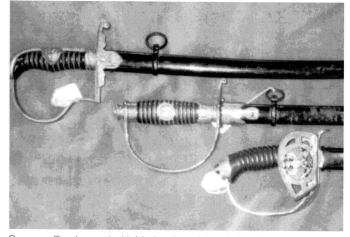

German officer's sword with Nazi eagle emblem. Prince Eurgen.
WWII period. **£495**
S.S. officer's sword by Herman Rath, Solingen, Germany **£1,150**
Imperial German cavalry officer's sword **£160**

FIREARMS

A huge variety of weapons ranging from antique pocket pistols to modern submachine guns can be found at military collectors' events worldwide – proof of mankind's continuing fascination with firearms despite the best efforts of legislators.

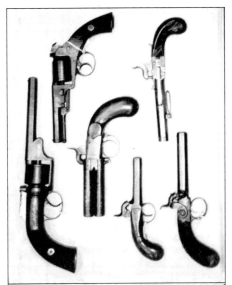

Today's collectors, hedged about with licensing restrictions, adverse publicity and moralising, must look back in envy to the days when the only restriction on gun ownership was the ability to pay the price asked by a gunsmith.

From the golden period of firearms development in the late 17th, 18th and 19th centuries come some of the finest antique weapons on the market today. Among the most rare and valuable are wheellock pistols which pre-date flintlocks, beautifully inlaid with ivory, mother of pearl and precious metals, and only to be found at the most prestigious collectors' events and auctions. More commonly encountered are military and civilian flintlock and percussion pistols. Among civilian weapons, duelling pistols, carrying an aura of romance and intrigue, are extremely popular, especially those by the foremost London makers such as Manton, Durrs Egg and Twigg. The more mundane military issue weapons are also in demand as they are generally dated and marked with the Tower or royal cypher and can be associated with particular campaigns.

For those seeking something a little different there are many unusual items to be found, dating from an era when lawlessness was widespread. Miniature pistols designed to be concealed in a lady's muff or pocket, pepperpot pistols, even ring pistols can be found as well as a variety of unconventional combination weapons such as knife and knuckleduster pistols. Reproductions are encountered among these curious weapons, so buyers are advised to purchase from a reputable source.

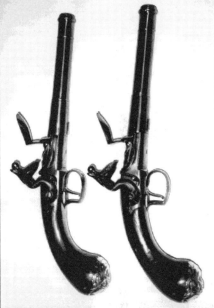

In the mid-19th century Colonel Samuel Colt is generally credited with having produced the first pistol to fire more than one shot without reloading. The Colt Naval revolver of 1851 is extremely collectable as are those made by manufacturers such as Remington, Adams and Tranter.

Among the longarms, the Brown Bess musket which armed British soldiers for almost a hundred years is still a best-seller. Sturdy and reliable, although lacking the accuracy of the Baker rifle which armed the British light infantry of the Napoleonic Wars, the Brown Bess was superseded by the Enfield percussion rifle, the Snyder cartridge rifle and the Martini-Henry of Zulu War fame, all of which are eagerly purchased by collectors today.

For specialists in First World War items, the Lee Enfield rifle is a popular choice and not too expensive. Also highly collectable from this period are Lewis, Vickers and Maxim machine guns.

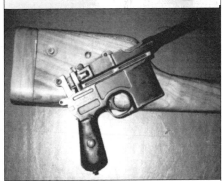

The move towards tighter gun controls is seriously depressing the UK market for more modern firearms. Changes in the laws regarding deactivation of weapons and what constitutes an 'antique' or obsolete firearm have also affected prices. For example, some semi-automatic weapons, such as M1 carbines and MP40s deactivated in the UK prior to November 1995, are now increasing in value because they still have moving parts, whereas later deactivation requires a dummy bolt welded into position. Similarly, the Martini-Henry rifle was removed from the firearms register in the UK two years ago and is no longer required to be deactivated. Those that were deactivated prior to this are therefore less valuable than a functioning specimen.

Before purchasing any firearm, other than an obvious antique, collectors are advised to investigate whether they require a licence.

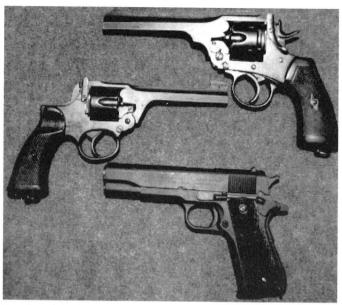

Deactivated pistols: Webley MKI .455 . . . . **£115**
English Tanker .38. . . . . **£85**
Colt M1911A1 .45 . . . . **£250**

9mm Mauser model 1898 semi-automatic pistol, 11½" overall, tubed barrel 5¼", rearsight to 1000m, flat sided hammer with larger hole, ribbed wood grips with traces of figure "9". WO & QGC, worn overall, action weak, brazed patch at breech in a modern walnut holster/stock with leather harness and cleaning rod **£460**
9mm FN Browning Hi-power semi-automatic pistol, 8" overall, barrel 4¼", adjustable rearsight, chequered varnished wood grips. GWO & clean . . . **£190**
6 shot .455" Webley mark VI DA service revolver, 11½" overall, barrel 6", the frame dated 1918, bearing various inspectors' stamps, chequered black hard rubber grips stamped with "S". GWO & clean condition, retaining most original finish with a khaki lanyard **£120**
6 shot .357" Magnum Smith & Wesson Mod 686-4 DA hand ejector revolver, 11½" overall, barrel 6", ribbed top flat with adjustable rearsight, stainless satin finish, Hogue Monogrip oversize soft rubber grips VGWO & near VGC . . **£210**
6 shot .38" S & W Special Smith & Wesson Mod 14-4 DA hand ejector target revolver, 11½" overall, barrel 6", matted top flat with adjustable rearsight, broad ribbed trigger and hammer spur, Pachmayr oversize soft rubber grips. VGWO & condition **£185**

East German AK 47 . . . . **£295**
U.S. M1 Garand. Shortened for use by paratroopers **£380**

Pair of flintlock pocket pistols by Mallett of London, circa 1800 . . . . **£950**
Mid 19th century game counters (Norfolk Liars) . . . . **£350** & **£450**

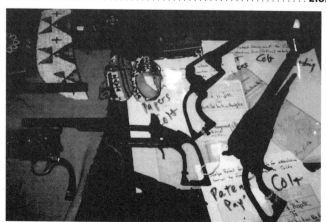

Relic pistols dug in Western American sites . . . . **US $75 – $300**

FURTHER READING

Robert Elgood, Firearms of the Islamic World
(I. B. Tauris & Co.).

Richard Law and *Peter Brookesmith,*
The Fighting Handgun (Arms and Armour Press).

John D. Walter, Secret Firearms (Arms and Armour Press).

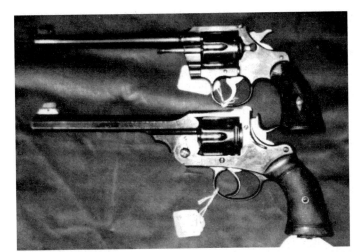

Colt officer's model 1912 . . . . **£650**
Webley WG 1914 . . . . **£800**

Double barrelled percussion shotgun 1860 by Armitage & Walker, with powder flask, shot flask, capper, oil bottles etc. **£750**

Belgian Montegrin Gasser. Just over 11mm. Dated 1890 . . . . **£450**

500 Gibbs rifle with walnut stock, with unusual action, circa 1870 . . . **£3,500**

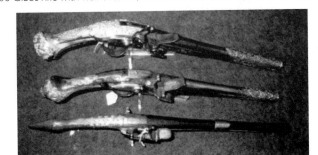

Turkish flintlock 1780 . . . . **£875**
Turkish flintlock 1780 . . . . **£295**
Balkan Miquelet 1750 . . . . **£345**

A selection of non-deactivated long arms, mostly Enfields. Priced from . . . . **US $75 – $275**

U.S. 300 Winchester Rifle, modified by Accuracy International in Portsmouth UK, contains many refinements and used by NATO forces . . . . . **US $6,000**

Guards dress sword, William IV period **£80**
Calisher and Terry capping breech loader **£625**
Cased pair or pocket percussion pistols, rifled, Fishenden, Tonbridge. Includes accessories **£495**

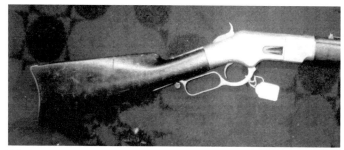

Winchester model carbine 1866, calibre 44 Henry rimfire, popularly called the "Yellow Boy" because of the brass frame. The Americans used to say "It was the rifle you loaded on Monday and shot all week". **£2,600**

Adams pistol. 51 Dragoon pistol .38 bore. Manufactured circa 1852-53. Typical of officer's British sale piece, 85% of original finish. **£750**

Deactivated pistols:
Luger **£200**
Mauser 9mm . . . **£250**
Belgian Browning
9mm. **£200**

Manhatten .36 calibre revolver, retaining 80% of its original finish **£750**

Top: British Long Enfield LEI by L.S.A. & Co. .303 calibre, fitted with a Tippings patent sight, circa 1890. As used in the Boer War and at the turn of the century **£350**
Below: Arisak Japanese Mauser 6.5mm action rifle, model 1899/05 38th year type, Imperial Japanese Army. **£185**

45 Colt Peacemaker with ivory grips . . . . **US $1,500**
French revolver. . . . . **US $450**
Remington percussion pistol. . . . . **US $500**
Holster, mittens and patch from WWI. **US $385**
Silver inlaid spurs. . . . . **US $250**

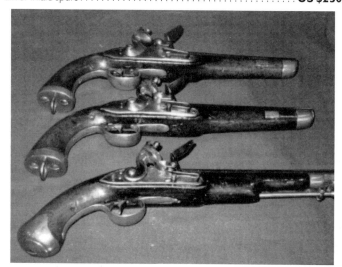

2 Belgian service pistols 1820/30 each **£360**
English Newland pattern pistol 1813-14 . . . . **£750**

Brown Bess 1805 musket **£575**

1860 London Colt Army 44 rimfire revolver with Richards cartridge conversion with shoulder stock **£2,600**

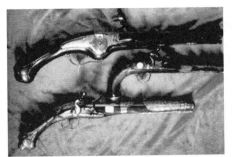

German wheellock military pistol from the
17th century **£2,500**
Ketland holster pistol 1780 .... **£390**
Middle Eastern flintlock pistol, circa 1800 . . . **£485**

A selection of rifles including a rare Westley-
Richards self-capping carbine with Damascus
barrel, walnut stock, complete with loading tools
in butt cap **£2,500**

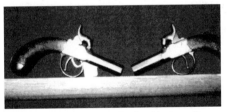

Pair of percussion pocket pistols with turn off
barrels and brass frame, German silver mounts,
circa 1840. Birmingham proofed. The pair. . . . **£475**

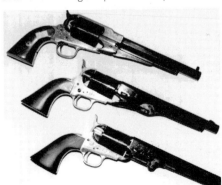

De-activated Remington **£195**
Blank firing Colt 1860 .... **£125**
Blank firing Engravers Colt 1851 .... **£125**

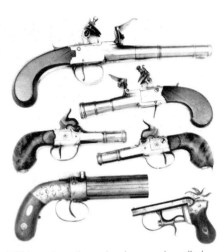

A 22 bore brass framed and cannon barrelled
boxlock flintlock holster pistol by Waters & Gill,
10¾" London proved, maker's tamped crowned
I.W. Border engraved frame with Waters & Gill
London in script. Sliding top thumb safety, flattened
walnut butt, oval silver escutcheon engraved JC.
Good working order (age worn overall, light pitting,
barrel lug removed, reaffixed at muzzle) . . . **£400**
A brass framed and barrelled flintlock boxlock
blunderbuss pistol, 7", flared barrel 3". Tower
private proofs. Frame script engraved Twigg
London. Sliding top thumb safety, concealed
trigger, flattened walnut grip. Good working
order, (some age wear overall) **£600**
An unusual pair of brass framed brass barrelled
boxlock percussion pocket pistols, 6" half
octagonal barrels 2½". Frames border engraved
with geometric roundels, hammers with flat
backed spurs. Rounded burr walnut butts with
shell shaped hinged cap box covers, possibly
E. European. Good working order **£410**
A 6 shot .28" Allen & Thurber self cocking
percussion pepperbox revolver, 7¼" fluted
barrels 3¼" stamped Allen & Thurber Worcester
Patented 1837 Cast Steel. Foliate engraved round
steel frame, bar hammer stamped Allen's
Patent.2 Piece wooden grips with oval WM
escutcheons. Good working order and condition
(some moderate pitting to barrels)....... **£280**
A scarce 80 bore DB Belgian Delvigne's Patent PF
pistol, 10.5cms, swivel octagonal barrels 7.5cms,
Liege proved stamped Delvigne Bte. SGDG 32.
Border engraved frame, button plunger trigger,
trigger guard pulls off to double as ejector rod.
Two piece chequered wooden grips. Good
working order and condition, (one action AF,
retains approx 50% original blued finish) . . . **£410**

MAB Model D pistol with Nazi markings **£85**

Three Barrelled tap-action flintlock by JNW
Richards of London, circa 1810. .... **£1,095**

French military pistol, converted to percussion in
1840s. No maker's marks – in nice condition.
Dated 1807, calibre .700 .... **£425**

Inert weapons, Fowling piece **£160**
Thompson SMG. **£175**
L1A1 British **£285**
Belgium F.A.L. **£185**
Steyr MP34 .... **£175**
Chinese RPG 2 .... **£75**

Percussion pistol. with belt hook. VGC **£310**

British Colonial Baker pattern
flintlock musket **£375**
Baker sword bayonet................... **£89**

Flintlock sporter by Durs Egg London 1790 . . . . **£830**
Flintlock holster pistol by Shuter, London 1760 . . . . **£695**

Mark I Bren gun .303. New and unused, complete with transit case, cover, mags etc. Dated 1941 . . . . **NPA**

French flintlock rifle with very unusual safety catch, circa 1770 . . . . **£590**

Percussion revolvers from the American Civil War. Percussion pepperbox revolvers, flintlock holster pistols, flintlock duelling pistols. **£1,000**

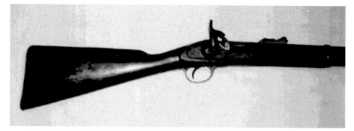

British Enfield Infantry musket, dated 1859. Early pattern, with spring retained bands. Lock marked with Crown, V.R. and Tower, with socket bayonet . . . **£385**

Various pistols, including a Tokarev 7.62mm Semi-automatic pistol **£135**

A selection of American small calibre rimfire pistols, used by gamblers and tricksters in the 1870s . . . . **£100 - £400**

Smith & Wesson Model 1½ .32 rim fire. Nickel circa 1890s **£375**
1860 Colt Army Civil War U.S. marshals .44 calibre revolver. . . . . **NPA**

Powder flasks from **£45**
Powder and shot measures from **£15**
Percussion cap dispenser **£175**
1870 rim fire revolver **£110**

Cased mid 19th century pin fire revolver by Le Faucheaux of Paris with original accessories . . . **NPA**

Cased pair of officer's belt pistols flintlock by Tatem & Egg, circa 1801-1814. Excellent working order and condition . . . **£3,400**

.22 Marlin lever action rifle. **£150**
Inert percussion fowling piece **£160**
De-activated flintlock blunderbuss. **£180**

U.S. flintlock pistol by Simon North, model 1816. . . . . **£900**

.303 Bren Mk 1M light machine gun, WWII dated. Mint condition **£185**

Wheellock rifle with rifled barrel, 1590-1610 very early model **£4,750**

Cased Colt pistol complete **£950**
Allen wheellock pocket revolver **£185**

Moores Patent .32 calibre 6 shot teat-firing revolver Pat. D 1864 . . . . **£225**
80D Adams patent 5 shot DA percussion revolver by Dean. London circa 1855 . . . . **£190**
7mm 6 shot pinfire revolver circa 1870 . . . . **£65**
7mm Guardian American MOD 1878 6 shot pinfire revolver **£125**
5mm pinfire revolver circa 1870 . . . . **£75**
German Fritum 8 shot blank fire revolver. . . . **£55**

German MP 34 Steyr Solothurn submachine gun. Waffenamt stamped, WWII dated, fine condition. Bayonet £29. . . . . **£199**

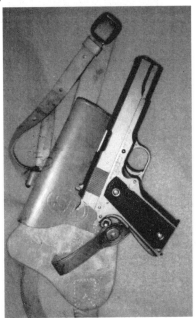

WWII de-activated Colt 45 in leather case, in mint condition **£285**

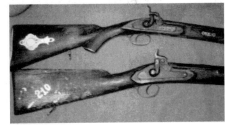

Hunting musket, muzzle loading 1860-70 . . . **£45**
Muzzle loading musket made for the Indian Militia **£45**

British Daystate Competa pre-charged air pistol complete with carrying case and accessories **£365**

Rare silenced British Sterling L2A3 submachine gun, designed for use by commandos. Fine condition... **£330**

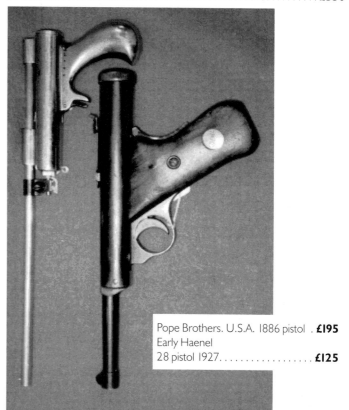

Pope Brothers. U.S.A. 1886 pistol . **£195**
Early Haenel
28 pistol 1927................... **£125**

British de-activated signal pistols
WWII **£65**
WWI **£95**
WWII 1½ aircraft fitting. **£95**
WWII English Schermilys **£85**

1993 dated Rumanian 7.62mm AKMS Kalashnikov assault rifle.
Bayonet £25 . . . . **£295**

Turkish blunderbuss **£45**

Allen patent 1837
.31 calibre pepperbox
cased revolver. Retailed
by Canfield
and Bros. Baltimore,
circa 1845 - 50 . . . **£900**

66' Winchester (Yellow Boy) . . . . **US $4,200**
Marlin Rifle – marked Atkinson, Topeka and Santa Fe Railroad . . . **US $1,095**
94' Winchester Saddle Ring carbine. . . . . **US $495**
76' Winchester .45 – 60 . . . . **US $1,895**

MG42 & Tripod. Battlefield relic in very good condition **DM2000**

WWI Ribbed Vickers machine gun **£475**

Coonan .357 American magnum automatic which also fires .38, special adjustable rear sight for windage, stainless steel **£475**

LARTI 9mm Swedish pistol, with holster and cleaning kit. Post WWII . . **£175**

British Sterling Mk 4 L2A3 submachine gun with folding metal stock **£225**

Webley MkIV .38 4" barrel with blued finish, WWII period.
De-activated or to shoot **£95**

WWII German Diana Model 30
Military training air rifle **£157**

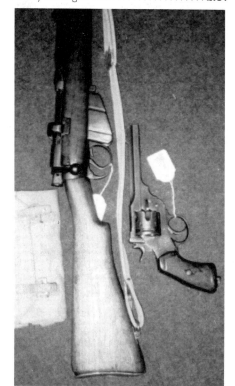

Bren Gun cleaning and stripping tool pouch
WWII dated **£3**
1916 SMLE No1 MK3 .303 Rifle **£170**
Webley Mk6 .455 revolver 1918 . . . . **£190**

Arabian percussion musket,
mid 19th century **£150**

Civil War carbine by Sharps and Hankin, cap and
breech mechanism. This model was for Navy use
and is the least common version.
Dated 1863 . . . . **£650**

French flintlock rifle sporting gun, 1750-1790 with
safety catch and rifled barrel **£550**

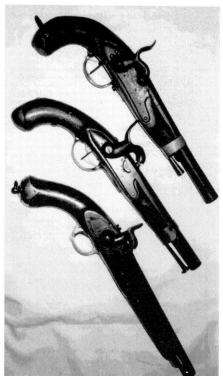

Spanish percussion belt pistol, circa 1845 . . . **£300**
French percussion pistol converted from a flintlock,
originally 1815, converted 1845 . . . . **£395**
Belgian percussion sea service pistol,
circa 1850 . . . . **£295**

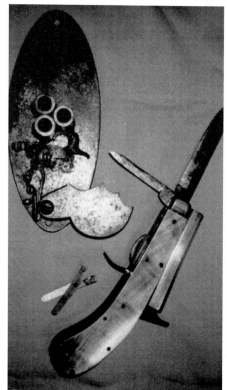

English penknife pistol by Unwin & Ridgers with
bullet mould, circa 1850 . . . . **£450**
Belt pistol, popular in India as defence against
Thugees. Worn on the back of the belt, from where
it could be fired at attackers approaching from
behind, circa 1840 . . . . **£400**

Selection of deactivated weapons. No. 4 . . . **£100**
C2 58 . . . . **£175**
P.PS. 41 . . . . **£195**
M16 (blank firing) **£265**
MP.44 . . . . **£285**

Battlefield relics including MP40 . . . . **DM400**
G41 + sniper scope **DM1,500**
K98 . . . . **DM200**

American rimfire cased pistol. Made in 1878 by
the Norwich Arms Co. **£450**

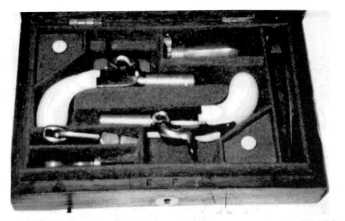

Pair of ivory handled cased muff pistols, circa 1840 . . . . **£1,400**

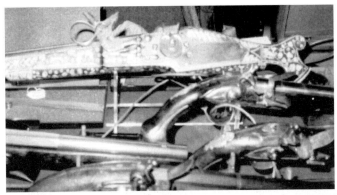

Wheellock pistol with inlaid bone stock **£6,500**

Nazi German 7.92mm MG 34 light machine gun. Waffenamt marked, excellent condition **£325**

Double barrelled flintlock gun made by Boutet of Versailles reputedly for Napoleon. Boutet made guns for Louis XVI & George IV. It has Damascus barrels and a short French walnut stock **£6,750**

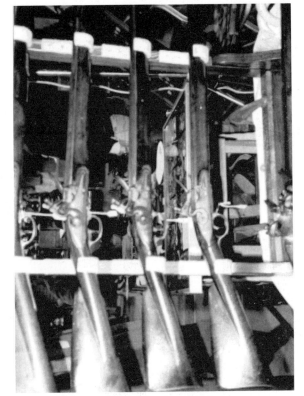

Brown Bess muskets from the Napoleonic war period . . . . **NPA**

De-activated pistols: Colt 1911 . . . . **£225**
H&K ZP70 . . . . **£300**
Mauser Bolo **£250**
Colt .38 . . . . **£75**
Mauser stock **£130**

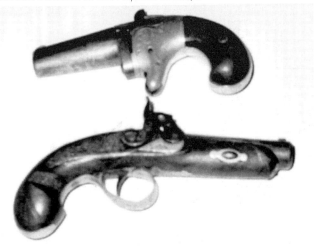

Two Derringers, National Army Derringer Model No2 .41 rim fire . . . **£400**
Derringer percussion .44 pistol with German silver mounts and a walnut chequered stock **£500**

East India Government percussion holster pistol, circa 1871.
Indian Armoury marking on barrel **£450**
English officer's holster pistol to the Notts Light Horse by Tatham & Egg.
Brass mounted, circa 1790 . . . . **£650**

Webley air pistols from . . . . **£40 – £85**

Swiss MGII calibre 7.62mm machine gun circa 1938. Thought to be the only one in the UK, with its own optical sight by Zeiss, original water can and hose, and an ammunition box with belted link, plus spare barrel box **£1,650**

Top: English .38 bore Tranter by Calesher & Terry with 1851 patent . . . **£750**
French 8mm St. Etienne revolver 1895 . . . . **£345**
American Colt series II revolver. Post WWII **£925**
.32 Smith & Wesson tip up barrelled rim fire revolver, circa 1875 . . . . . **£305**
Lastly, an antique Galand Velodog .230 revolver, which was carried by cyclists travelling through Belgium or France at the turn of the century. Small enough to keep in a pocket, it was used to shoot at dogs snapping at riders' heels. **£225**

WWI Mark I Vickers heavy machine gun with corrugated jacket. **£495**

A selection of replica western pistols from **£30**

German 17th Century wheellock holster pistol, unusually scalloped decoration to the lock plate. From the 30 year war. **£2,800**
English combination pistol-knife by Unwin and Rogers. **£395**
English iron cottage tinder lighter, circa 1760 . . . . **£385**

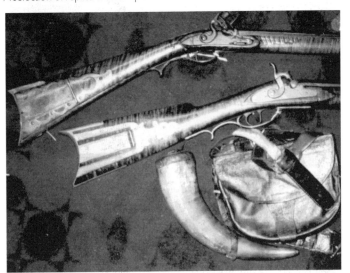

Top: Kentucky flintlock rifle by Fister of Bedford County, circa 1790 . . **£1,500**
Middle: Percussion Kentucky, circa 1840 . . . . **£850**
Bottom: Mountain man's hunting bag, powder horn and patch knife,
circa 1840 . . . . **£300**

WWII MkI Bren gun, dated 1942, with adjustable bi-pod legs,
including transit case **£150**

Extremely rare self-cocking revolver, made by The London Armoury
Company, retailed by B. Cogswell. The gun has 95% original blue and is
contained in its own maroon lined oak box with accessories,
circa 1857 . . . . **£1,345**

M38 C2 Pistol deactivated **£150**

Russian 1910 Maxim, used in the Finnish War in the mid 1930s and also used in WWII. 7.62 calibre and includes ammo can and mount **£595**

Cased William Egan (Bradford) percussion revolver, circa 1850, with cleaning brush, flask, ball mould and oil bottle **£1,150**

General purpose machine gun **£1,500**

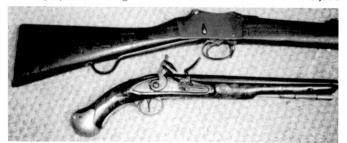

.557/45 bore Martini-Henry Mk IV B service rifle. Full ordnance proof to breech. Crisp Enfield V. cypher dated 1888. Two piece walnut stock. Butt with Enfield roundall and regimentally marked "K YR/112". Barrel and action has 75% blue with excellent bore **£460**
65 calibre fullstocked flintlock G.R. Sea Service Pistol. Circa 1790 to 1805. Lock stamped with Crown G.R. cypher and Tower barrel. 12" Tower proof marks to breech. Brass furniture. Original belt hook. Wooden ramrod is later. Top saw screw missing. **£850**

P 14 sporting deactivated rifle **£175**

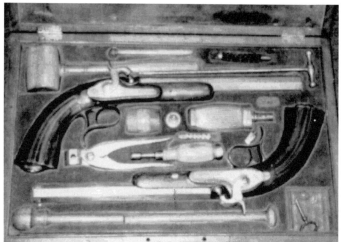

Walnut cased percussion duelling pistols. With micro-groove rifling. Made by Jalabert Lamotte of St. Ettienne. Complete with accessories. **£3,750**

American WWI Smith & Wesson **£200**
British Webley, 1918 to 1940s, with holster **£150**
German broomhandled 9mm Mauser 1900 to 1918 . . . . **£230**
German Luger, WWII dated 1941 . . . . **£225**

ORDNANCE

Artillery has been a fundamental part of warfare since the mid-14th century when the devastating power of gunpowder began to replace the arrow-storm of medieval battle tactics. Like the early First World War tanks, its effects must at first have been morale-boosting rather than cataclysmic, as the unreliability of early field pieces meant that they could be as fatal to friend as to foe.

Over the centuries, the potential of artillery has been refined and developed from cannon firing crude but effective lead balls and shot to guns firing the enormous range and diversity of shells and projectiles which are available to today's fighting forces. However, without the ammunition, cannon, fieldguns, tanks, howitzers and the like are just so many pieces of expensive scrap metal, and for an increasing number of collectors worldwide, it is the ordnance or ammunition rather than the gun itself which excites interest.

One possible reason why this should be so is the comparative wealth of inert ammunition to be found at very moderate cost. Many collectors whose budgets do not run to cased sets of flintlocks, early Colt pistols or Winchester rifles, or who simply do not have the space for a field piece or howitzer, have turned to collecting inert small arms ammunition.

In the mid-19th century the race to develop cartridge-based ammunition and the weapons to fire it took off. Great inventors with a flair for engineering, ballistics and originality – Hotchkiss, Armstrong, Whitworth and companies like Colt, Remington, Krupp and Vickers – all threw their hats into the global ring and the result was the arms race. Each gun, whether capable of being held in the hand or pulled by a train, needed ammunition. The invention of rifling, breech loading, driving bands and shell cases containing detailed information provided the incentive for interested parties to gather together examples of ammunition by country, calibre or type.

While some enthusiasts will collect anything that could be fired from a gun, others specialise in particular aspects of ordnance. The opportunities are extensive: small arms ammunition, fuses, shell cases, grenades, mortars, armour-piercing projectiles, dummy/drill rounds made of hardwoods and brass, training rounds, inert examples 'borrowed' from factories or engraved by grateful employers for faithful service, a souvenir of the battlefield sometimes engraved with details of where and when it was found and even occasionally with details of who found it... all these can form the basis of historically interesting and valuable collections.

Although they may not need an unlimited budget, ordnance collectors do need diligence, contacts and luck, for experienced collectors know that they cannot simply acquire their more unusual pieces from an auction catalogue or dealer's list. They must go out in search of them and then have the enjoyment of research and identification. Brass shell cases which found their way back home as souvenirs and ended up as doorstops or repositories for nothing more lethal than umbrellas or cigarette ash, can still be picked up at car boot or garage sales and junk shops as well as at collectors' events. It is worth keeping an eye open for good reference material, which is also important.

Here, perhaps more than with any other aspect of militaria collecting, safety is an important issue and the wise collector will make sure that everything he handles, acquires or exchanges is completely inert ... the only injury it can then cause is by dropping it on a foot.

Various artillery shells and mortar bombs, from . . . . **£10 – £60**
i.e. Far left: British 81mm firing practice mortar bomb. **£28**
Far right: British 4.5 naval shell, fairly modern **£60**
Next to above: British tank proof round. 105mm **£50**

German PAK.H.E. 37mm shell 1941. . . . . **£55**
Russian A.P (armour piercing) round 40mm. 1944 dated **£55**
Czech A.P.H.E. shell 37mm. 1938. . . . . **£55**
USSR 30mm A.P.H.E. shell 1960 . . . . **£15**
U.S. H.E. shell 37mm 1942 . . . . **£50**
German WW2 20mm H.E. aircraft cannon. 1940 dated. **£50**
German WW2 20mm Brandt round 1940 . . . . **£15**

Modern British 30mm Harrier Jump Jet
Aden shell cases **£2**
Complete round **£5**

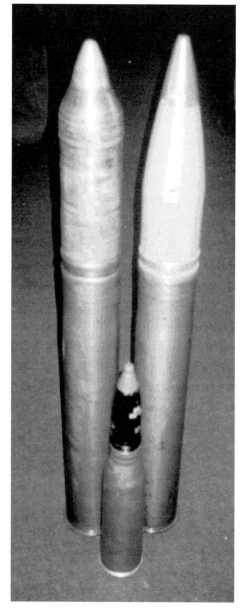

10.5cm German WW2 illuminating round, dated 1942. . . . . **£24**
WW2 German 10.5cm H.E. round, dated 1941 . . . . **£240**
Russian A.P.H.E. 57mm round 1983 . . . . **£85**

British Paratrooper's mortar, complete in original box **£120**

Reproduction cannons, large **£175**
Small **£15**

WW1 German egg grenade, complete with wire pull and detonator **£30**

British WW1 18 pounder artillery shells, brought back from France. Full of lead balls, each **£25**

Rubber batons (or bullets) as used in Northern Ireland or for riot control **£4**

Tips for collectors

If at all possible never acquire a case that has been in the sea or is so black and dirty from being buried that it is impossible to see what the surface is like. Over time the constituent parts of brass separate out and instead of having a brass shell case the collector will end up with one covered in a red copper deposit impossible to clean off.

British modern
30mm shell **£6**
British modern
20mm shell **£6**
British modern
20mm shell **£6**

 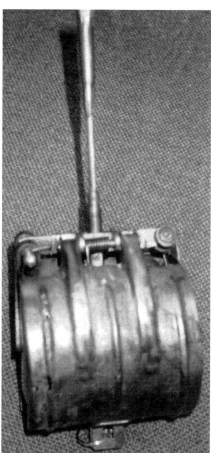

Left: WW2 German 88mm round **£165**
Right: German WW2 4 propeller butterfly bomb. **£140**

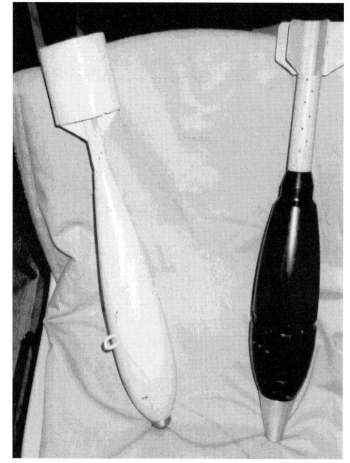

British WW2 25 pound aircraft practice bomb usually dropped by Beaufort
bombers . . . . **NPA**
British 75mm mortar round. H.E. 1970s . . . . **NPA**

FURTHER READING:
Terry Gander and Peter Chamberlin, Small Arms Artillery and
Special Weapons of the Third Reich. Pub by Macdonald & Janes.

Ian V. Hogg, German Artillery of World War II
Arms and Armour Press

A late Georgian iron cannon on its original iron carriage, barrel 29½" bore
diameter 1¼" turned reinforces, swollen muzzles, integral trunnions, swollen
cascabel. Pierced iron carriage with 4 solid cast wheels, iron elevating screw.
Standing on mahogany plinth. **£400**

French M57 rocket launcher. Mid 1950s. **£165**

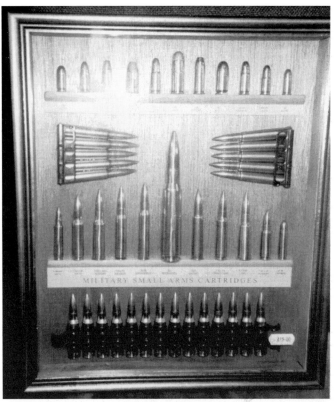

MILITARY SMALL ARMS CARTRIDGES

Cased WW2 British military small arms collection. **£95**

WW1 German, French and British shells. L to R:. . . . **£25, £25, £20, £18, £50**

Box of 12 British Mills grenades, inert. Price per box. **£350**

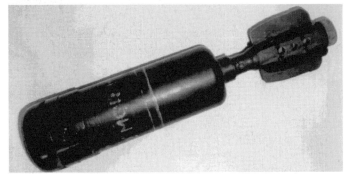

British 2" mortar bomb, 1939 to 1950s. Used by British troops throughout the world **£15**

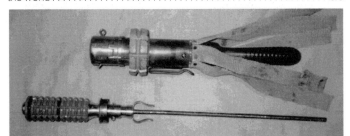

Left: WW1 British Hales grenade Mark II **£75**
Right: WW1 British Mark II hand grenade **£150**

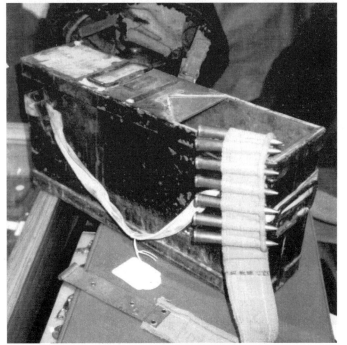

.303 Vickers 250 rounds. Patented 1942.
10 x .303 1944. . . . . **£40**

A pair of garden cannons. £195

WW2 British Piat. £120

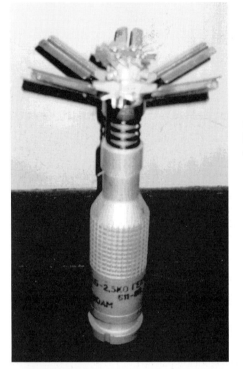

Russian anti-personnel bomblet a P-TAB. Current issue £75

Left: WW2 German Panzer Faust 60 anti-tank gun £250
Right: British "Toffee Apple" mortar WW1 . . . . £55
German WW1 grenades, large size. £22
Small. £15

WW2 Italian Clinometer for a field gun,
with wooden box. £45

FURTHER READING:
British and American Artillery of World War II
Arms and Armour Press

The Illustrated Encyclopaedia of Ammunition
Apple Press

The Illustrated Encyclopaedia of Artillery (Apple Press).

Naval Gun *by John Batchelor*. Published by Blandford Press).

British Artillery Weapons and Ammunition 1914–1918.
by L. F. Thurston. Published by Ian Allen 1972.

12" reproduction cannon.. . . . . **£175**

Colonel Wade demolition charge for bridge demolition. **£3**
Russian 7.62mm machine gun ammunition box – repainted and re-issued for
Iraq/Iran war. **£15**
84mm Karl Gustava anti-tank missile. **£20**

WW1 fuses from the Somme: left to right, top row. British 60 pounder. . . **£8**
German 1916 8 pounder. **£8**
German 1916 8 pounder. **£8**
British 60 pounder. **£8**
Middle row: French 75mm. **£8**
French 75mm **£8**
German 1915 H.E. **£6**
English No. 88. . . . . **£6**
Bottom row: No. 44 fuse, English, dated April 1916. . . . . **£10**
English 18 pounder. **£4**

U.S. post war
3.5 inch
Bazooka. . . **£150**

British fuse setting kit. **£15**

WWI German stick grenade, practice model. Good condition, contains porcelain ball and pull cord **FF220**

Top row: .45 for U.S. Auto Colt Pistol. **50p**
British drill rounds 7.62mm. **50p**
U.S. .30 cal MI Carbine.. . . . . **50p**
Middle: A U.S. Garand 30.06 clip of eight. **£8**
British clip of five .303. . . . . **£5**
Below: .455 for British service pistol. **50p**
.9mm Browning High-power. **50p**

Left: WWI grenade, possibly French **£28**

Right: British WW2 Mills grenade **£45**

60mm mortar (possibly Italian). . . . . **NPA**

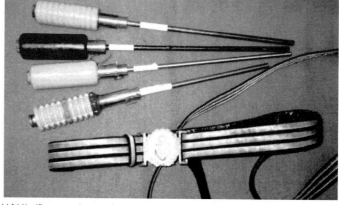

WWI rifle grenades, each **£50**
Royal Navy flag officer's sword belt. Kings Crown **£50**

WW2 British P.I.A.T. bomb.
Dated November 1944 . . . . . **£120**

Belts of fired 7.62mm ammunition in metal box, which were fired from
H.M.S. Yarmouth in the Falklands War **£12**

British WWI percussion grenade **£150**

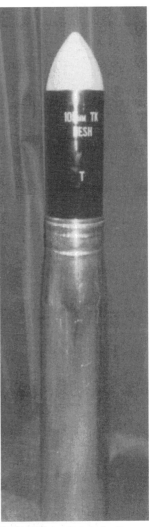

WW2 German incendiary bomb,
dated 1937 . . . . **£45**

British 105mm tank shell with
HESH (High Explosive Squash
Head) 1972. Manufacturers mark
RLB. (Royal Logistics Berkeley)
Unfired head **£150**

Tips for collectors

Watch out for cases which have been shortened. Always
make sure that the tops are even and smooth as
irregularities could indicate that someone has taken an
inch or two off the top to get the shell out leaving the
case less than its true length.

Check especially smaller calibre shells up to 18lb and 3"
diameter to make sure the driving band is original.
Original driving bands are 'sweated' onto shells and show
no join whereas replaced driving bands will show a
soldered joint.

MISCELLANEOUS

Every military collectors' event contains a variety of articles that do not fit into any specific collecting category and yet are often among the most fascinating and unusual items on the market.

Books, paperwork and reference material are essential to the collector who wishes to advance his hobby; so it is worth spending some time looking through boxes of pamphlets and photographs for interesting items. Government booklets on ordnance, weapons and equipment are a good buy while contemporary magazines, posters and newspapers help to provide background detail.

Especially popular at the moment are accounts of Special Forces in the Second World War, particularly the Paras, Chindits and Long Range Desert Force. Many of these accounts were written in the late 1940s and 1950s and such is the demand for these once neglected books that many are being reprinted. Reference books of all sorts, particularly those on specialised topics, usually have small print runs and quickly go out of print; for example, Adams Revolvers was remaindered soon after publishing in the 1970s but now commands £50 to £80 a copy.

Boer War and First World War stereoscopes containing unique 3D photographs occasionally turn up and are a worthwhile purchase. Postcards – from flimsy field cards to the beautifully decorated French and Belgian examples from the First World War – are prolific and inexpensive and can often provide useful uniform, weapon and equipment references.

First World War trench maps are worth searching for, especially maps associated with well-known battle areas such as the Somme or the Ypres Salient, as are the Second World War maps printed on silk for airmen.

Flags and banners, particularly Third Reich examples, command good prices as do Third Reich silverware, porcelain figurines and pottery such as decorated beer steins.

Zulu War artefacts – knobkerries, hide shields and spears – have enjoyed a revival of interest since the film Zulu and are perhaps the most collected of ethnic weapons, but there are also other interesting pieces to be found such as masks, knives and knuckledusters.

Death plaques – the engraved bronze discs issued with a commemorative scroll to the next of kin of First World War casualties – are seen at most UK collectors' events. They sometimes accompany medals and paperwork related to the casualty but are also collected in their own right.

Also very collectable are Zippo lighters dating from the Second World War onwards and marked with military crests. A good Vietnam example might fetch around £25.

FURTHER READING:
Forman's Guide to Third Reich German Documents and their Values
by Adrian Forman
Published by Bender USA

A Bibliography of Regimental Histories of the British Army
by Arthur S. White
Published by Naval and Military Press

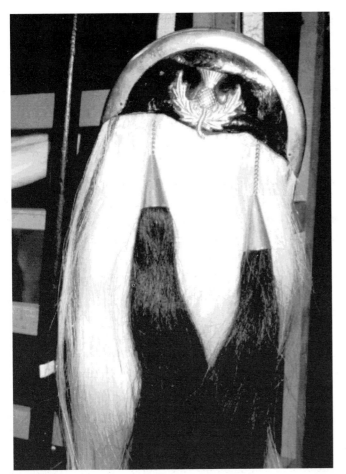

Other ranks sporran of the London Scottish **£20**

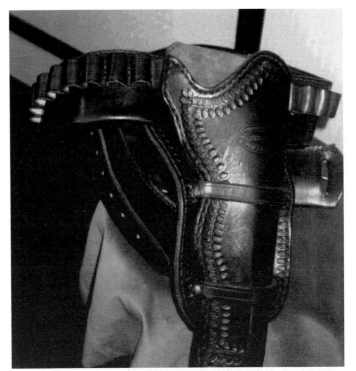

Leather hand-made holster and money/cartridge belt.
This is a custom-made example **£95**

U.S. entrenching tool, dated 1945, in canvas holder. **£12.50**

M16 furniture set **£15**

Tips for collectors

Regimental or Divisional histories are very popular and many command prices of £50-£200. It is important to check that they are complete. Many come with maps in pockets at the back which are often missing. Some with plates have them missing, having been torn out and framed by a previous owner. This type of damage can halve the value of a book, or even render it valueless for re-sale. It then becomes only of use to cannibalise to complete another damaged copy.

German powder flask, replica of a 17th century model. **£10**

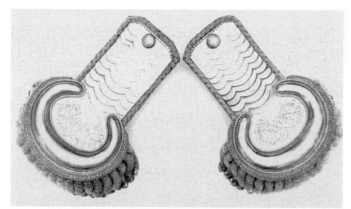

A good pair of officer's silver scale epaulettes of The 4th Royal Irish Dragoon Guards c1825. Embroidered border, 3" silver bullion tassels, applied gilt script "RIDG" and shamrock wreath within crescents, regimental button. Near VGC. **£680**

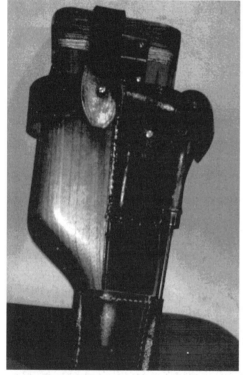

Broom handled holster/wooden stock for a Mauser **£125**

A typical example of a hand sewn straight cartridge belt and 7½ inch holster of the mid 1880's. Fully embellished with nickel studs, and to complement the set are matching cuffs. (These were worn to protect the wrists from rope burns when roping cattle). **£250**

Soviet Military commemorative pocket watches, 18 jewels, each. **£25**

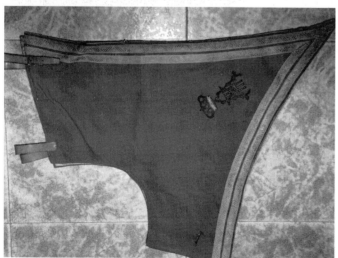

Bodyguard saddle of cavalry Alfonso XIII "Royal Guard" mod 1909-1931 . . . . **PTS 100.000**

Limited edition plates, Coalport, Wedgwood, Royal Doulton. WWII German and British aircraft. Priced each . . . . **£20 – £26**

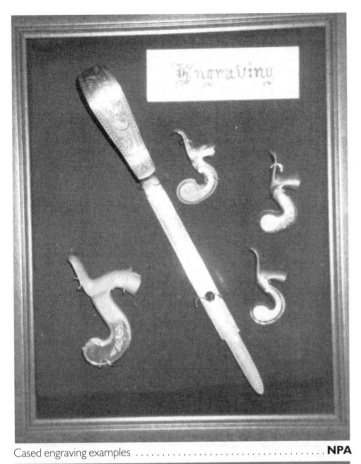

Cased engraving examples . . . . **NPA**

Brass and white metal pickelhaube plate,
circa 1890 . . . . **£30**

German 1939 dated
dinner service with
swastika. Includes
plates, coffee pots etc.
Prices for pieces
from . . **100 – 330 FF**

Plaque to Canadian Expeditionary Force, made locally in Britain to mark the
headquarters. Made in lead in wooden frame **£60**

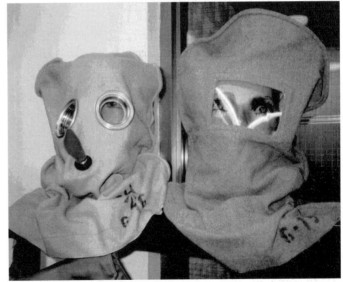

Reproduction WWI Hypo helmet P.H. smoke hood. Left: (inc bag) **£40**
Right: (inc bag) **£25**

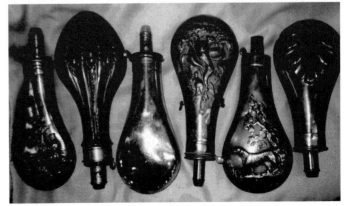

Powder flasks circa 1850, in copper, brass and nickel silver,
from. . . . . **£45 – £120**

Military prints and pictures and antique engravings.
i.e. "Scotland Forever" 3' x 2'. **£65**

Silver plated brass desktop ornament of VI flying bomb or "Doodle Bug" . . **NPA**

Kettle Drum skirt from the 3rd Division S.S. Deutschland Division, condition
near mint with identification markings etc. . . . . **US $10,000**

The stud draughts outfit dated 1915. (French draughts game) **£70**

Canadian stirrup and bridle **£20**
Imperial German Army wall drape **£400**

Tips for collectors

Serious book collectors will always go for hard backs with dust
wrappers in at least good, or better condition. If possible buy first
editions or author (or biographical subject) signed copies which will
increase in value.

WWII signal Heliograph MK5. Totally complete with original wooden tripod legs, dated 1943. Leather carrying case filled with all the necessary accoutrements, including spare mirror **£225**

Air Ministry Bell, as used on air bases. 1945 . . **NPA**

American cold weather masks WWII **£15**

German WWII Mercedes of Thüringen S.S. departmental typewriter. Has party badge on face and S.S. badge on lid. There is also a specific S.S. Key **£300**

Adolf Hitler's silverware, found at Führerball, Munich. All embellished with Hitler's initials and crest. Includes serving plates and dishes, plus cutlery, napkins, cigarette box etc. **$100,000**

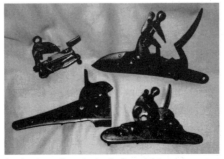

A selection of gun locks. Left to right:
Pattila Spanish pistol lock North Africa,
circa 1800 . . . . **£40**
East India Company musket lock,
circa 1800 . . . . **£50**
Green's carbine. Maynard tape primer 1860 . . . **£60**
Rare screwless lock by Henry Nock, London,
circa 1800 . . . . **£200**

Rum barrels as issued on board ship. All original
brasswork **£325**
Ship's anchor in solid brass **£450**
Ship's gimbal mounted compass **£350**

Bronze statue of Gurkha soldier WWI **£150**

Aluminium WWII prisoner of war cigarette case . **£8**
Matchbox holder. Nurse Cavell **£12**
Snuff box inscribed "In honour of Bradford
Territorials WWI **£35**
Lusitania Medallion. Issued in WWI to raise funds
after Lusitania was sunk by the Germans **£14**
A pair of copper vases. WWI trench art, inscribed
"Arras". Pair **£14**
Trench art shell case and bullets.
Royal Artillery badge **£14**

Mahogany, hand made, Special Forces plaque approx 3' high and 2' wide. Made in Vietnam in the 60s. . . . . **US $75**

A selection of brass and copper from the British Navy, R.A.F. and Army:
Ship's compass **£245**
Ship's whistle. **£75**
Diver's torch. **£75**
Searchlight from Green Goddess fire engine. 1950s **£230**
Inspection light **£65**

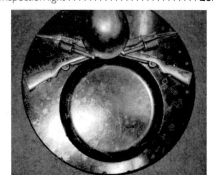

Commemorative ashtray with helmets, rifles and stick grenades.
WWII German marble and pewter **£75**

"The Dambusters" by Robert Taylor, signed by the seven pilots who survived the war **£350**

German serviette rings in tortoiseshell. Pair . . **£20**
French WWII dynamo torch. **£20**
British WWII helmet lamp **£10**
Spanish vendetta knife. 1930s **£45**

Imperial German ship's compass **£200**

Luftwaffe Banner, use unknown, with silk cording and tassels.
Size approx 2' wide by 3' high . . . . **US $125**

Early German Klein-Adler (2) typewriter.
Possibly 1930s **£40**

Horsehair bridles. Made at Yuma Prison, Arizona . . . . **US $NPA**

WESTERN FRONT RELICS

The battlefields of the First World War attract thousands of visitors each year just as they have done virtually since the last shots were fired. The mothers, fathers, wives and sweethearts who came at first to mourn their dead and to see for themselves last resting places, have given way to later generations of pilgrims, amateur historians and those seeking a clearer understanding of the conflict.

Whatever the motives for a visit, anyone who has walked the battlefields of the Somme and the Salient around Ypres, or visited Verdun or the Argonne will be aware of the large amount of relic items still to be found. There are those who would maintain that removing such relics destroys evidence for future generations but that argument is unlikely to carry much weight with the many collectors who are fascinated by the detritus of war. This desire to find something that has been lying undisturbed for eighty or more years is surprisingly infectious, and such is the atmosphere of some of the places that looking in the hedgerows or the ploughed fields becomes almost compulsive.

What is there to find? The answer is almost anything that was used both to make war and to make life supportable for the combatants – all sorts of equipment (entrenching tools, wirecutters, wire pickets, mess tins, rum jars and so on), weapons (rifles, bayonets, parts of tanks, gun carriages, machine guns), personal items (cap badges, shoulder titles, buttons, dogtags, boots), as well as ordnance by the ton. French and Belgian farmers are still reaping an 'iron harvest' as each new ploughing throws up its crop of dud shells and wire pickets. These can be seen piled at the side of the road awaiting collection by the authorities. Anyone tempted to investigate, however, should remember that the millions of shells fired so long ago are still claiming lives and limbs today.

First World War relic items can be purchased at most UK and European arms fairs as well as at several museums in France and Flanders, but there is nothing quite like discovering something that has remained hidden for generations and speculating as to what happened to its previous owner. By uncanny coincidence, a fortunate collector came across two halves of the same German dogtag on visits to one place separated by more than a year.

Road works are a good source of supply: the recently laid gas pipeline across the Somme battlefield yielded some interesting finds, as did the construction of a roundabout outside the town of Albert, where hundreds of rolls of barbed wire and other equipment were found.

Although First World War items are perhaps most prolific, relic items from other wars are also eagerly collected and can often be bought at collectors' events. Musket and cannon-balls from English and American Civil War battlefields, along with ancient weapons – even medieval arrowheads, have been seen recently. Those who lack the time or patience to search for themselves can always purchase the results of someone else's labours.

FURTHER READING:

The Somme Battlefields *by Martin and Mary Middlebrook*. Pub. by Penguin

•

Archeology of the English Civil War *by Peter Harrington*. Pub. by Shire Publications

•

Discovering Battlefields of England *by John Kinross*. Pub. by Shire Publications

Miscellaneous WWI items, various prices, includes British Mills grenades, British rifle grenade, water bottles and British WWI dated wire cutters priced at **£20**

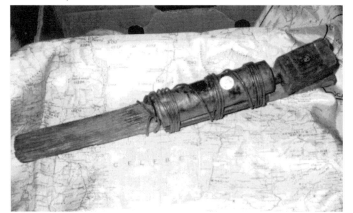

Early WWI French stick grenade **£28**

German water bottle, Lewis gun pannier, brass shell cases. British shovel, German shells, 2 British shells, billy can, cutlery and British 'toffee apple' bomb.

Just a few of the many rusty fuses which litter the battlefield

Collection of British and German buttons, name tags, belt buckle and whistle.

German wirecutters.

Spade, shovel, wire picket and stokes mortar.

British and German bottles.

Belt buckle thought to belong to a German Padre

A Manchester Regiment 'tram driver's' cap badge.

German M1916 pattern steel helmet found at Hawthorne Ridge crater.

Horseshoes, British and German grenades, pickaxe head, cutlery, stirrup and button cleaner.

British water bottle and jug.

German water bottle and cup.

British Lee Enfield rifles with bayonets still attached found at Gueudecourt whilst laying a gas pipeline. In the foreground can also be seen a British 'SRD' rum jar and spade.

French 'trench made' stick grenade. Typical of this type of 'home-made' grenade.

A British Lee Enfield rifle minus its rotted stock. Found near Beaumont Hamel.

British issue 'Service Rations Department' Rum Jar.

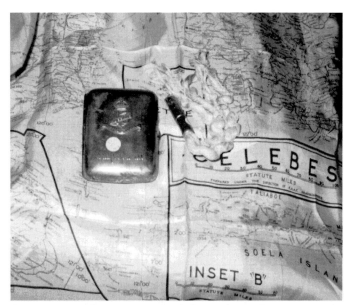

Cigarette case to 13th Hussars inscribed "Good Luck and Success presented by Robert Baden-Powell 1915" **£50**

German wirecutters found at Triangle Farm in Ypres.

Two French made stick grenades.

British 'Toffee Apple' bombs found in tunnels adjacent to the sunken lane, Beaumont Hamel.

Early design German stick grenade with side mounted firing lever **£120**

German trench mortar on display at a Belgian museum.

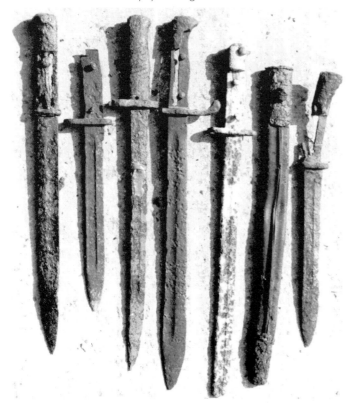

A selection of 'dug-up' bayonets and scabbard. Both British and German. The wooden handles have rotted away leaving just the skeleton of metalwork.

German trench mortar shell. Below, a German Luger pistol found at Beaumont Hamel.

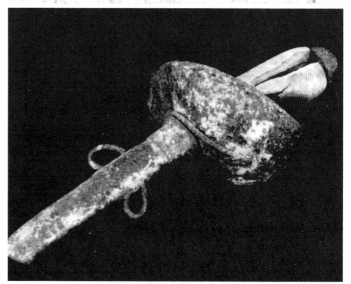

A British cavalry sword handle, still in its sheath but cut, probably by a farmer's plough. It was found at the edge of High Wood.

Relic German WWI grenades . . . . **50 FF**
Relic shell fuses . . . . **40 FF**

ARMS & MILITARIA FAIRS

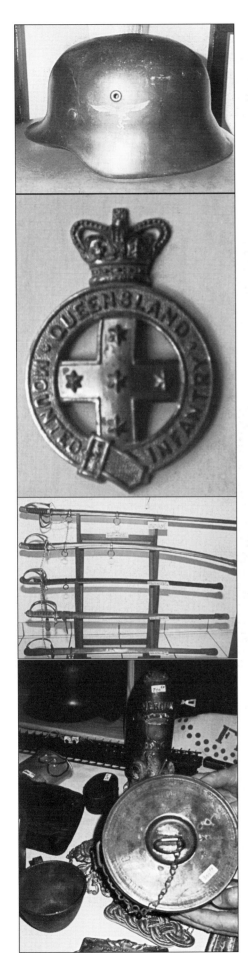

THE MAJOR UK ARMS FAIR ORGANISERS ARE:

- Arms Fairs Ltd. Tel: 01273 475959 – *The London Arms Fair.*

- Nigel Hill, Arms & Armour UK, 58 Harpur Street, Bedford MK40 2QT. Tel: 01234 344831– *Bedford and Dunstable Arms Fairs.*

- Antique Militaria & Sporting Exhibitions, PO Box 104, Warwick CV34 5ZG . Tel: 01926 497340 – *"The International", Birmingham.*

- Ron Sparks Militaria Fairs, PO Box 62, Sarisbury Green, Southampton SO31 5ZB. Tel: 01703 453418 – *regular fairs in nine venues in the south of England including Dorking and Farnham.*

- Mark Carter Medal & Militaria Fairs, PO Box 470, Slough SL3 6RR. Tel: 01753 534777 – *regular fairs in three venues, Aldershot, Gloucester and Chipping Sodbury near Bristol.*

- Holmes & Long. 96-98 Derby Road, Nottingham NG1 5FB. Tel: 0115 9474137 – *Nottingham Arms Fair.*

- Northern Arms Fairs. Tel: 01423 780940 – *regular fairs throughout the north of England including The Royal Armouries Museum in Leeds.*

- Trevor Whitehurst, SADACS. Tel: 0161 485 6908 – *Stockport Arms Fairs.*

- AJW Arms Fairs, PO Box HP96, Leeds, LS6 3XU. Tel: 0113 2758060 – *regular fairs throughout the north of England plus the Glasgow Arms Fair.*

- Sovereign Fairs. Tel: 01438 811657 – *regular fairs in the south of England including Sandhurst and Watford.*

- David A. Oliver. Tel: 01669 620618 – *the Park Lane Arms Fair, London.*

- Central Militaria Fairs. PO Box 104, Warwick, CV34 5ZG. Tel: 01926 497340 – *Winchester and Cheltenham fairs.*

- Military, Naval and Aviation Bookfairs. Tel: 01892 538465 – *military book fairs in London, Marlborough, York and Tunbridge Wells.*

- Ray Brough. Tel: 0181 776 0329 – *regular fairs in Tunbridge Wells, Wokingham, and Bromley.*

- Mr E. Kenten. Tel: 0410 393694 (mobile) – *monthly fair at Southgate, London.*

- Andrew Taylor. Tel: 0161 485 3908 – *two Cheshire arms fairs at Warrington and Macclesfield.*

- Colin Bardgett. Tel: 01768 890143 – *"The Borders" fair at Carlisle.*

- North Kent Military Collectors Society. Tel: 01634 375098 – *fair at Gravesend, Kent*

- John Burgess. Tel: 01782 394397 – *Stoke on Trent fair, Staffordshire.*

- Cannon Curios, 21 Bulford Road, Durrington, Wiltshire. Tel: 01980 655099 – *Stonehenge Militaria Fair.*

- H & B Medal Fairs. Tel: 0151 424 0630 – *Wakefield Medal Fair.*

- Mr F. Walland. Tel: 0181 590 4389 – *Britannia Medal Fairs.*

- Colin Tebb, Essex MVT. Tel: 01245 251857 – *annual Tilbury Fort Military Vehicle Show and monthly Tilbury Fort Militaria Fair.*

- Saga Arms Fairs. Tel: 0171 486 5223 – *Regents Park Arms Fair at Lord's.*

- Rex Cadman, The Old Rectory, Sandwich Road, Ash, Near Canterbury, Kent CT3 2AF. Tel: 01304 813128 – *the annual Beltring War and Peace Show.*

- Solent Military Vehicle Preservation Club Tel: 01705 250463 – *annual Overlord Show.*

- London Military Market, Camden Passage. Tel: 01628 822503.

- Dragoon Militaria. Tel: 01246 234837 – *Bolsover Castle fair, Derbyshire*

ARMS & MILITARIA FAIRS

SOME WORLDWIDE MILITARY SHOW CONTACTS:

• Eddie Wyer, 87 Cardonagh Park, Donaghmede, Dublin 13, **Ireland.** Tel: 01-8479100 – *Irish Militaria Fair,Dun Laoghaire.*

• Thierry Gourlin, Musée des Abris, Rue Anicet Godin, Albert, Somme, **France.** Tel: 322. 75. 16. 17 – *Albert Arms Fair.*

• A.V.A.M., Boulogne, **France** Tel: 03.21.30.40.72 Fax: 03.21.30.40.00 – *Boulogne Arms Fair.*

• Daniel Langlet, Ytres, Somme, **France** Tel: 321.73.32.73 – *Sailly Saillisel and Peronne Arms Fairs, Somme.*

• Normandie Expositions Tel: 02.35.77.34.59 – *Evreux Arms Fair, France.*

• A. Archen, **France.** Tel: 01.60.04.61.00 – *Mas Baltard, Paris.*

• Irmgard Maier, Dr.-Dahlen-Strasse 12, D-76089 Bad Dürkheim, **Germany.** Tel: 06322-2786 – *Deidesheim Arms Fair.*

• Messe Stuttgart International, Am Kochenhof 16, D-70192 Stuttgart, **Germany.** Tel: 0711-2589-373 – *Stuttgart International Arms Fair.*

• Expo Management, Wolf Krey, Rosenweg 4, D-24133 Molfsee, **Germany.** Tel: 0431-650608 – *Berlin, Frankfurt and Nuremberg International Arms Fairs.*

• Westfalenhallen Dortmund GmbH, Rheinlanddamm 200, D-44139, Dortmund, **Germany.** Tel: 0231-1204-521 – *Dortmund Arms Fair.*

• Leo Watermeier, 3800 Taft Park, Metairie, Louisiana 70002, **USA.** Tel: 504.887.6709 – *Greater New Orleans Military Show.*

• Terry Patton, Box 441175, Kennesaw, Georgia 30144, **USA.** Tel: 770.419.7897 – *Marietta Militaria Show.*

• Steve Johnson, PO Box 4706, Aurora, Illinois 60507, **USA.** Tel: 630.851.0744 – *Chicago and Dallas Military Shows.*

• Thomas Johnson, PO Box 350, Moorstown, NJ 08057, **USA.** Tel: 609.866.8733 – *Military Antiques Xtravaganza (MAX).*

• Charles Snyder, 3520 Mullin Lane, Bowie, MD 20715, **USA.** Tel: 301-262-5735 – *Baltimore Arms & Militaria Show.*

• Betty Marquette, PO Box 43, Branford, Fl 32008, **USA.** Tel: 904-935-2342 – *Florida Arms & Militaria Show.*

• Donna Harris, 8900 N. Vancouver Ave, Portland, OR 97217, **USA.** Tel: 503.283.2940 – *Portland Military Collector Show.*

• Texas Military Collectors Association, PO Box 550742, Dallas TX 75355-7042, **USA.** Tel: 214-341-4196 – *TMCA Military Exposition.*

• Frank Galati, PO Box 10, Wesco, MO 65586, **USA.** Tel: 573-775-2308 – *Collinsville Military Collectibles Show & St Louis Gun & Knife Show.*

• Ohio Valley Military Society, PO Box 1115, Cincinati, Ohio 45201-1115 **USA.** Tel: 513-542-5880 or 513-481-8104 – *Show of Shows, Louisville, Kentucky.*

• Vintage Productions, 400 W. Alondra Blvd, Gardena CA 90248, **USA.** Tel: 213-770-4444 – *San Diego Militaria Show.*

• Carolina Trader Promotions, Box 769 Monroe, NC 28111-0769, **USA.** Tel: 704-282-1339 – *Carolina Military Antiques Show.*

• Livio Cillo. Tel: 410-836-3572 – *Pikesville Collectible Arms, Swords & Militaria Show, Baltimore, USA.*

• William Price, Tennessee Militaria Collectors Assoc, Box 1006, Brentwood, Tennessee 37024, **USA** – *Tennessee Military Show.*

• Tony Daws, Graton Enterprises, P.O. Box 80153, Green Bay, Auckland, **New Zealand.** Tel: +64 09 817 4074 – *Aukland Militaria Show.*

INDEX